W9-BKG-815

THE

CHESS DOCTOR

BRUCE PANDOLFINI

A FIRESIDE BOOK
Published by Simon & Schuster
NEW YORK   LONDON   TORONTO   SYDNEY   TOKYO   SINGAPORE

FIRESIDE
Rockefeller Center
1230 Avenue of the Americas
New York, NY 10020

FIRESIDE and colophon are registered trademarks
of Simon & Schuster Inc.

Designed by Stanley S. Drate/Folio Graphics Co. Inc.

Manufactured in the United States of America

10 9 8 7 6 5 4 3 2

Library of Congress Cataloging-in-Publication Data

Pandolfini, Bruce.
    The chess doctor : surefire cures for what ails your game / Bruce
Pandolfini.
        p.   cm.
    "A Fireside book."
    Includes index.
    1. Chess problems.   I. Title.
GV1451.P354   1995
794.1'7—dc20   95-36679
                                                        CIP

ISBN 0-684-80121-3

Contents

Introduction   *17*

On Reading Chess Moves   *19*

PART · ONE

THE OPENING

DEVELOPMENT

1 Falling behind in development   *30*

2 Developing aimlessly   *32*

SELF-BLOCKING

3 Blocking your own forces   *34*

4 Locking bishops inside the pawn chain   *36*

5 Blocking the queen-bishop with the
queen-knight   *38*

OVERUSE

6 Overusing the queen   *40*

7 Moving the same piece several times   *45*

8 Making too many pawn moves   *48*

CENTRALIZATION

9 Abandoning the center   *53*

10 Developing knights to the edge ... 55

11 Developing knights only to the second rank ... 57

12 Bringing the queen to an assailable center square ... 60

13 Surrendering the center to the enemy queen ... 62

14 Missing a fork trick ... 65

ATTACK AND DEFENSE

15 Letting the initiative slip ... 70

16 Attacking prematurely ... 72

17 Aping your opponent's moves ... 74

KING, ROOK, AND CASTLING

18 Delaying castling or not preparing it ... 76

19 Letting your king get trapped in the center ... 78

20 Allowing a check that takes away your right to castle ... 80

21 Moving rook to queen-one instead of castling queenside ... 83

22 Castling into danger ... 85

23 Castling on the wrong side ... 87

24 Castling and losing a pawn ... 89

25 Castling into a pin ... 91

26 Castling into a skewer ... 93

27 Failing to connect the rooks ... 96

28 Not keeping your king in the center for the endgame ... 98

BISHOP'S PAWN

29 Moving the f-pawn unwisely   *103*

30 Not moving the f-pawn out of fear   *106*

31 Blocking the c-pawn in certain openings   *109*

BISHOP PINS AND FIANCHETTOS

32 Automatically playing B-N5 to attack a knight   *111*

33 Creating a self-pin with an enemy bishop on knight-five   *115*

34 Placing a bishop where it can be driven back by pawns   *117*

35 Failing to complete a fianchetto   *121*

36 Flanking and self-trapping the other bishop   *124*

PART · TWO

CAPTURES, RECAPTURES, AND EXCHANGES

TRADING WHEN AHEAD OR BEHIND

37 Trading when behind in material   *128*

38 Avoiding advantageous trades when ahead in material   *130*

39 Trading pawns when you should be trading pieces   *132*

40 Trading pieces when you should be trading pawns   *134*

RECAPTURING

41 Taking back with the wrong unit   *136*

42 Taking away from the center   *138*

43 Taking automatically to straighten one's pawns   *140*

44 Taking back with a pawn and obstructing a key square or line   *142*

TENSION AND THE INITIATIVE

45 Trading when it's better to maintain a tense situation   *144*

46 Delaying a capture when unfavorable tension should be ended   *146*

47 Letting the opponent take first   *148*

48 Trading and thereby surrendering a file   *150*

49 Automatically opposing rooks   *153*

50 Trading a developed piece for an undeveloped one   *155*

51 Aimlessly trading and dissipating your attack   *157*

52 Avoiding a useful trade and forfeiting the initiative   *159*

53 Automatically taking to double opposing pawns   *162*

54 Taking a pinned unit instead of piling on   *165*

55 Trading and freeing your opponent's game   *167*

56 Letting your opponent trade off a bad piece   *169*

57 Letting your opponent trade off a weakness   *171*

KING CONSIDERATIONS

58 Automatically taking with check   *173*

59 Missing the opportunity to capture with check   *175*

60 Surrendering a fianchettoed bishop to win a pawn   *177*

61 Taking the e-pawn at the wrong time   *179*

PHOBIAS

62 Fearing to recapture on Q4 with the queen   *181*

63 Arbitrarily avoiding a queen trade   *183*

64 Trading only to have less material on the board   *185*

PART · THREE

MISTAKES WITH SPECIFIC UNITS

PAWNS

65 Moving pawns heedlessly   *190*

66 Placing your pawns on the same color as your bishop   *192*

67 Making foolish moves to avoid doubled pawns   *194*

68 Moving rook-pawns carelessly   *196*

69 Creating the wrong escape square   *198*

70 Moving pawns that shield your castled king   *200*

71 Pushing the wrong pawn when mobilizing a majority   *202*

72 Unnecessarily relinquishing a two-square option   *204*

73 Exposing the seventh rank   *206*

KINGS AND ROOKS

74 Ignoring the oppositional relationship between the kings   *208*

75 Failing to activate the king   *210*

76 Moving the wrong rook   *212*

77 Letting your rook become passive   *214*

78 Missing the cutoff   *217*

PART FOUR

GENERAL PLAYING ERRORS

PLANNING

79 Playing without a plan   *220*

80 Staying with a plan too rigidly   *224*

81 Giving unnecessary or pointless checks   *228*

82 Playing for cheapos   *230*

83 Moving instantly because your opponent is short of time   *232*

84 Moving too quickly   *234*

SELF-INFLICTED WOUNDS

85 Unnecessarily putting your pieces in pins   *236*

86 Letting enemy units camp out in your position   *238*

87 Relying on a vulnerable unit   *243*

88 Self-trapping your own pieces   *245*

MATERIAL CONCERNS

89 Holding on to material unreasonably   *247*

90 Making too many queens   *249*

91 Grabbing pawns   *251*

92 Taking unnecessary material   *253*

93 Sacrificing without good reason   *255*

94 Declining a refutable sacrifice out of fear   *257*

MISPLAYING ATTACK AND DEFENSE

95 Falling into stalemate   *259*

96 Allowing unnecessary counterplay   *261*

97 Failing to encourage your opponent to go
     wrong   *263*

98 Missing the chance to cut your losses   *265*

99 Missing a saving possibility   *267*

100 Resigning prematurely   *269*

APPENDICES

A   Tactics Glossary   *271*

B   Tactics Index   *275*

C   Sacrifice Squares   *277*

Index   *279*

To Joe Pandolfini,
for all the reasons

Acknowledgments

This book would not have been possible without the efforts of a dedicated team, including Bruce Alberston, Carol Ann Caronia, Deirdre Hare, Rob Henderson, Burt Hochberg, Idelle Pandolfini, and Larry Tamarkin, all of whom made valuable contributions to the book's content and appearance.

Introduction

The Chess Doctor is a book of practical advice. It diagnoses and treats the mistakes made in typical chess games—not all errors, just the most common.

One hundred characteristic ailments are offered, such as falling behind in development, moving the wrong rook, and resigning prematurely; each followed by a discussion of the ailment, how it arises, when it occurs, why we allow it, and so on.

For each ailment there is an "Rx," with numbered recommendations to help readers avoid the ailment, watch out for it, or minimize it. You'll even find ways to inflict the malady on less wary opponents and how to plague them further once they already have it.

Following the Rx are one or more diagrams with analysis. This pattern—ailment, discussion, Rx, diagram, and analysis—is sustained throughout. The material is arranged in four sections: the opening, captures, mistakes with specific units, and general errors. The diagramed examples come from actual games, some quite famous, or were created for didactic purposes.

All the examples are analyzed in algebraic notation. You'll also encounter a discussion of descriptive notation, along with a conversion chart to enable you to switch from one system to the other. You may ask why I have used both notation systems in the same book. Actually, I haven't. Familiarity with algebraic notation is all you need to follow the examples. But because some concepts are actually better understood by referring to them descriptively, I chose in some cases to use descriptive names for reinforcement. Descriptive nomenclature is explained in the notation section.

Despite the current popularity of algebraic notation, descriptive notation still has a place. Consider this: Is it better to talk about the problems of the a- and h-pawns or the problems of the rook-pawn? Is it more elegant to speak about b- and g-file play or knight-file play? Is it clearer to recommend attacking f7 when you have White and f2 when you have Black, or simply to suggest focusing on king-bishop seven? In all three instances, the second expression, the descriptive one, is more natural and more readily understood.

This doesn't mean I recommend descriptive over algebraic notation. To record chess games I prefer the less ambiguous algebraic. But to teach chess, to express concepts generally as well as accurately, I prefer a mixture of both, with a reliance on algebraic.

As for the Rx's, they tend to be generic and broad. While they don't provide a strict set of instructions for correcting a problem, they should have a constructive influence on your play, reinforced by periodic reading and review over time.

A final admonition. Chess is endlessly creative. So be careful about following any of these suggestions too rigidly or beyond reason. Exceptions make chess a fascinating game, and generalizations may fail when applied to specific circumstances. Remember that principles are general guidelines, nothing more. They can hint at a solution, but if you follow them inflexibly, they become the problem.

Educators tend to inundate students with advice and countless rules of thumb. These are propounded to start students up the right avenues. In the end, the best advice is aimed at inspiring them to solve their own problems, to think for themselves. This is the role of a dedicated teacher.

On Reading Chess Moves

You will get more from this book if you can read chess notation. There are two types of notation: algebraic and descriptive. *The Chess Doctor* uses algebraic notation to present its chess moves, but it also uses descriptive names in some cases, so you should familiarize yourself with what follows.

Algebraic Chess Notation

To understand algebraic notation it's necessary to view the board as an eight-by-eight grid. Every square on the grid has its own name, derived from the connecting files and ranks.

Files, the rows of squares going up and down, are lettered **a** through **h.** Ranks, the rows of squares going across, are numbered **1** through **8.**

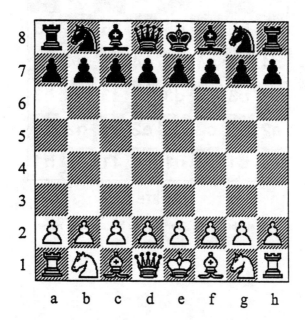

The starting position.

Squares are designated by combining those letters and numbers. For each name, the letter is lowercase and always appears first, before the number. Thus, in the diagram of the starting position, the White king occupies **e1** and the Black king **e8.**

There is only one perspective in the algebraic system: White's. All squares are named based on the White side of the board. For example, the a-file is always on White's left and Black's right. The first rank is always the one closest to White and farthest from Black.

The algebraic grid below gives the names and positions of all the squares. You might find it helpful to photocopy the grid and use it as a bookmark so it's always there for review.

BLACK

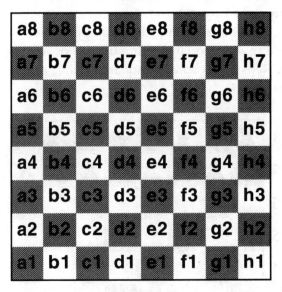

WHITE

The algebraic grid. Every square has a unique name.

Other Symbols

You will find it useful to learn the following symbols used in chess notation:

Symbol	Meaning
K	king
Q	queen
R	rook
B	bishop
N	knight
P	pawn
−	moves to
X	captures
+	check
#	checkmate
0–0	castles kingside
0–0–0	castles queenside
!	good move
?	bad move
!!	brilliant move
??	blunder
!?	probably a good move
?!	probably a bad move

Note that although **P** stands for pawn, it is not used in algebraic notation (its use will be seen in the explanation of descriptive notation to follow). If no indication of the moving unit is given in algebraic notation, the move is a pawn move.

A Short Chess Game

Consider the following short chess game, consisting of three moves for White and three for Black. Each move is diagrammed and given in algebraic notation.

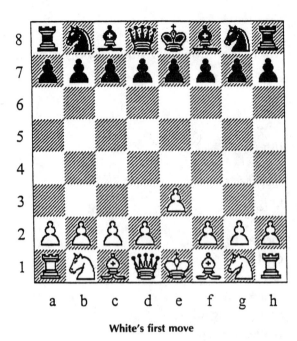

1. e3
"pawn to e3"

White's first move

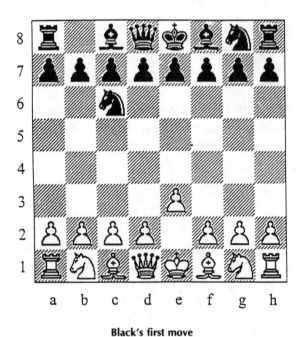

1. . . . Nc6
"knight to c6"

Black's first move

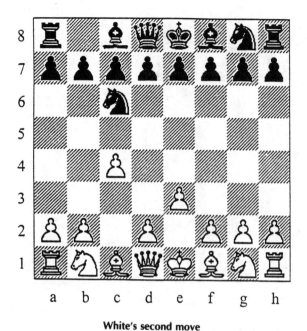

2. c4
"pawn to c4"

White's second move

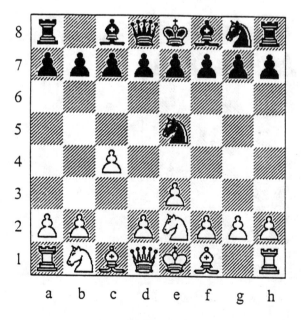

2. ... Ne5
"knight to e5"

Black's second move

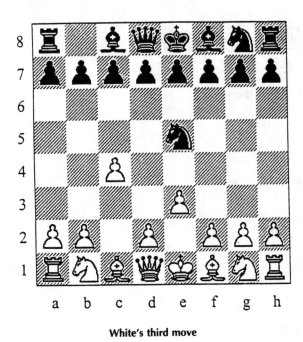

3. Ne2
"knight to e2"

White's third move

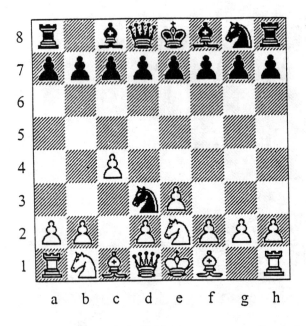

3. . . . Nd3#
"knight to d3 mate"

Black's third move

In chart form these moves would appear like this:

	White	Black
1.	e3	Nc6
2.	c4	Ne5
3.	Ne2	Nd3#

Or in sentence form:

1. e3 Nc6   2. c4 Ne5   3. Ne2 Nd3#.

Descriptive Chess Notation

In the descriptive system, squares are named by referring to the names of the pieces rather than to the letters a–h, as in algebraic. Furthermore, each move is recorded from the perspective of the player making it, whereas in algebraic only White's perspective is used. When White makes a move, both players record it from White's point of view; when Black moves, both players record it from Black's perspective. The following diagram shows the descriptive names of the squares.

									Black
8	QR8 QN8 QB8 Q8				K8 KB8 KN8 KR8				1
7	QR7 QN7 QB7 Q7				K7 KB7 KN7 KR7				2
6	QR6 QN6 QB6 Q6				K6 KB6 KN6 KR6				3
5	QR5 QN5 QB5 Q5				K5 KB5 KN5 KR5				4
4	QR4 QN4 QB4 Q4				K4 KB4 KN4 KR4				5
3	QR3 QN3 QB3 Q3				K3 KB3 KN3 KR3				6
2	QR2 QN2 QB2 Q2				K2 KB2 KN2 KR2				7
1	QR1 QN1 QB1 Q1				K1 KB1 KN1 KR1				8
White									

The names of the squares in descriptive notation.

Using descriptive notation, the same three-move game would appear this way in chart form:

	White	Black
1.	P-K3	N-QB3
2.	P-QB4	N-K4
3.	N-K2	N-Q6#

Or in sentence form:

1. P-K3 N-QB3   2. P-QB4 N-K4   3. N-K2 N-Q6#.

These six half-moves would be spoken as:

(1.) "pawn to king three" (P-K3); "knight to queen-bishop three" (N-QB3); (2.) "pawn to queen-bishop four" (P-QB4); "knight to king four" (N-K4); (3.) "knight to king two" (N-K2); "knight to queen six, mate" (N-Q6#).

File Conversions

Algebraic Names	Descriptive Names
a-file	queen-rook file
b-file	queen-knight file
c-file	queen-bishop file
d-file	queen file
e-file	king file
f-file	king-bishop file
g-file	king-knight file
h-file	king-rook file

Rank Conversions

Descriptive notation from White's point of view uses the same names for the files as algebraic notation. The first rank is White's first rank, the second rank is White's second rank, the third rank is White's third rank, and so on. But in descriptive notation, White's first rank is Black's eighth rank, White's second rank is Black's seventh rank, White's third rank is Black's sixth rank, and so on.

One area of confusion concerns the concept of the seventh rank, as in the maxim: rooks belong on the seventh rank. The "seventh rank" in this case is independent of algebraic notation. It is a descriptive use of the term, signifying the seventh rank from the point of view of either player.

PART•ONE

THE
OPENING

1

AILMENT:

Falling behind in development.

The main battle in the opening is a battle of time, based on two concepts: the initiative and development. White takes the initiative with the first move. Black tries to blunt White's initiative and then to seize it. The other aspect of time, development, concerns getting the pieces to effective squares as expeditiously as possible.

Generally, the more pieces you have out, the better your development and the sooner you can begin your attack. If you fall significantly behind in development, you will be playing catch-up for the rest of the game, if the game lasts very long at all.

Rx

1. Develop quickly, with concerted purpose.
2. Aim to develop a different piece on each move.
3. Find the best square for a piece and get it there.
4. Lag behind at your own risk.
5. Frustrate your opponent's development if it doesn't cost you.
6. Play practice games in which you try to activate all your pieces in the first twelve moves.

1

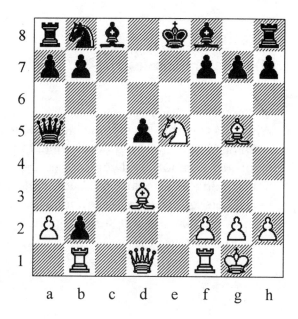

In this position from the game Keres–Winter, Warsaw 1935, White has sacrificed three pawns for a tremendous lead in development. Black finally activated his king-bishop with **1. . . . Bd6**, but White was able to cash in his time edge by **2. Nxf7!**.

The game concluded **2. . . . Kxf7 3. Qh5+ g6 4. Bxg6+! hxg6 5. Qxh8 Bf5 6. Rfe1 Be4 7. Rxe4! dxe4 8. Qf6+**, and Black resigned (1-0).

Mate would follow either **8. . . . Ke8 9. Qe6+ Kf8 10. Bh6#** or **8. . . . Kg8 9. Qxg6+ Kf8 10. Qxd6+ Kg8 11. Qe6+ Kg7 (11. . . . Kh7 13. Qf7+) 12. Bf6+** and so on. Black's lack of development was his downfall.

2

AILMENT:

Developing aimlessly.

While it's true that developing pieces logically in the opening is good, any old development for development's sake is not. If all your pieces are out but are not working as a team, you'll accomplish nothing. Several pieces cooperating toward a particular goal, such as checkmate, will surely topple a full enemy army in disarray.

Rx

1. Don't develop your pieces just to get them off the front row.
2. Consider where to put each one ahead of time.
3. Develop all your pieces harmoniously and supportively.
4. Be sure none of them interferes with your other forces.
5. If a deployment seems too early, wait for a better time.
6. For the openings you count on, learn where all the pieces usually go.
7. During games, close your eyes when it's not your move and imagine how to complete your development.
8. Practice doing this in study sessions.

2

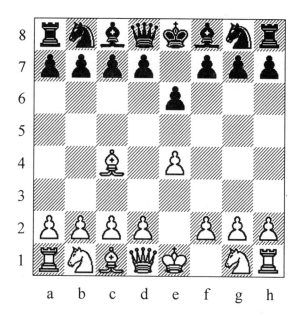

BLACK TO MOVE

In Problem 2 (after the moves **1. e4 e6   2. Bc4?**), White's second move develops his king-bishop aimlessly. The bishop might do well on c4 if it had a clear line to f7, as in some double king-pawn openings.

But against the French Defense (1. e4 e6) such a placement is pointless. The bishop strikes at a pawn wall and will have to move again after **2. . . . d5   3. exd5 exd5.** Play it then to b5, and even though it's check, more time will be wasted after c7-c6.

This is reminiscent of another desultory start, 1. e4 e5   2. Bb5?. The rebuffing 2. . . . c6 immediately compels the bishop's withdrawal. It also gains Black a clear diagonal for his queen (a5-d8) while supporting a subsequent d7-d5. Don't develop for development's sake. A placement should be sensible for the situation at hand.

3

AILMENT:

Blocking your own forces.

If you develop minor pieces—especially bishops—in front of your own center pawns, you won't be able to complete your development satisfactorily. You'll either have to resort to a forced fianchetto to get out the other bishop (and its companion rook), or you'll have to move the impeding bishop once again and then advance the center pawn. This wastes moves that could be used to marshal other pieces. In addition to retarding development, blocking a center pawn deprives your position of coordination. Finally, the inability of one center pawn to move means the other one might be harder to defend.

Rx

1. Don't block center pawns when developing pieces.
2. Don't retreat pieces so that they block center pawns.
3. Plan to place pieces so they don't encumber.
4. Try to figure out optimal placements for all units before moving any of them.
5. Don't be overly rigid. Accept an awkward development to avert greater problems.
6. Modify your ideas as the game proceeds and necessity calls.

3

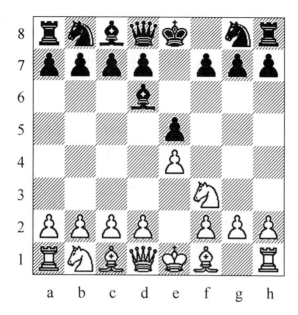

WHITE TO MOVE

The position of Problem 3 was reached after **1. e4 e5   2. Nf3 Bd6?.** While this last move doesn't lose immediately, it impairs Black's ability to complete his development, for now the d-pawn is blocked and useless. If Black doesn't want to waste a tempo moving the dark-square bishop again, he will have to resort to a queenside fianchetto to extricate the c8-bishop, which is an unnatural placement in most double king-pawn openings.

With either 3. d4 or 3. Bc4, White nurtures a growing advantage. Better for Black is either 2. . . . Nc6, 2. . . . d6, or 2. . . . Nf6, none of which retards development.

4

Locking bishops inside the pawn chain.

One of the problems with moving center pawns only one square is that such placement might block the diagonal of an unmoved bishop, thus preventing it from occupying a more aggressive square, say at QB4 or QN5. Black, being a move behind White, often has to settle for an obstructive move with his d-pawn. In both the Queen's Gambit Declined (1. d4 d5 2. c4 e6) and the French Defense (1. e4 e6), for example, Black's e-pawn obstructs his queen-bishop. Generally, hindering a bishop's development *unnecessarily* is deleterious.

Rx

1. Try not to block your bishops with your center pawns.
2. Develop your bishops outside the pawn chain.
3. Keep them inside only if the situation or opening setup recommends it.
4. Before moving a center pawn to its third rank, consider the resulting formation with regard to the scope of your bishops.
5. If you must block your own bishop with a center pawn, keep an eye out for a possible exchange of the piece.
6. If so blocked, look for freeing advances.
7. Even if a piece is hampered, use it.

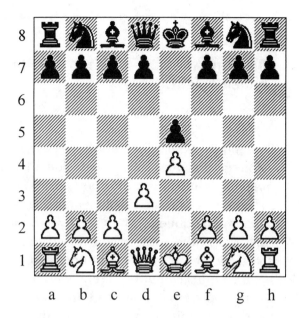

BLACK TO MOVE

The setup moves of Problem 4 are **1. e4 e5 2. d3.** White's last move doesn't lose, or even give Black the advantage, but it's certainly not the most aggressive way to handle a double king-pawn opening, where White's leitmotif is the two-square advance of the d-pawn.

In order to play his queen-pawn to d4 now, White must waste a move. Meanwhile, the mobility of White's light-square bishop is hampered until d3-d4 is achieved. Instead of 2. d3, White gets more mileage from either Ng1-f3, Nb1-c3, Bf1-c4, or f2-f4, and none of these hinder development.

AILMENT:

Blocking the queen-bishop with the queen-knight.

Sometimes your queen-bishop has a clear developing diagonal but you decide to place your queen-knight in front of it on Q2. This may be appropriate in certain situations: in many openings blocking the queen-bishop is only temporary, especially when the game has a closed or semi-closed character, and the QB might not need to be developed so quickly. But be careful with this, for it cuts the bishop's protection of K3. In open positions especially, exploiting tactics against this QN/QB encumbrance abound.

Rx

1. Don't unnecessarily obstruct your QB with your QN.
2. Before developing a knight to Q2, determine if your opponent has a bishop sacrifice on your KB2.
3. Be especially sure that he can't follow with a nasty knight check at your KN4.
4. If this stratagem exists, consider castling before it could happen.
5. If your knight is already on Q2, see if you can move it gainfully, restoring the QB's hold on K3.
6. Judge whether it's desirable to develop the QB before developing the QN to Q2.
7. Master the art of preventive thinking. Anticipate problems ahead of time.

5

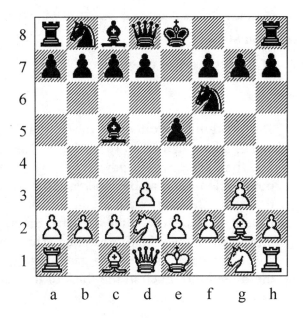

BLACK TO MOVE

Problem 5 arises after **1. g3 Nf6   2. Bg2 e5   3. d3 Bc5   4. Nd2?.**

White's queen-bishop no longer guards e3, thanks to the QN's blocking development. The winning score comes with **4. ... Bxf2 +!   5. Kxf2 Ng4 +**, and White is in a quandary.

If he retreats his king to e1 or f1, the knight invades on e3 and wins the queen. And if White continues 5. Kf3, then 5. . . . Qf6 +   6. Kxg4 d5 +   7. Kh5 Qh6 is mate. White's problems stemmed from his fourth move, Nb1-d2, which cut the QB's juice along the e3-h6 diagonal.

6

AILMENT:

Overusing the queen.

The powerhouse queen is by far the most gifted piece, so it's natural to reach for it when trying to find the next move. Its power, however, is not without problems and responsibilities. The queen is not the game. Misuse can get you in trouble quickly. Unless tactics allow otherwise, the queen must be moved to safety when threatened. This costs time, a valuable commodity at the game's start. Immerse the queen too much in the thick of things and you might even lose it.

Rx

1. Don't bring the queen out too early.
2. Put your lesser units to work.
3. If you must use the queen, take exceptional care.
4. Avoid variations that are queen-dependent unless they're clearly advantageous.
5. Think of the queen as a last resort.
6. Attack your opponent's queen if it comes out too soon.
7. To learn how to employ the queen, first master its component pieces, the rook and bishop.
8. In practice games, whenever you think of moving the queen, look for a better move with a different piece.

6a

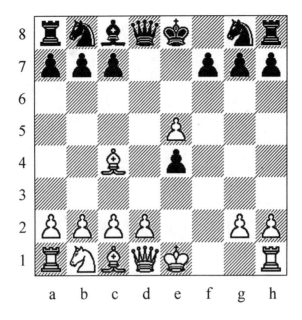

WHITE TO MOVE

This position occurred in the game Anderssen–Schallop, Berlin 1864, after **1. e4 e5 2. f4 d5 3. Nf3 dxe4 4. Nxe5 Bd6 5. Bc4 Bxe5 6. fxe5.**

Black now tried to win a pawn by using his queen, **6. . . . Qd4,** forking White's c4-bishop and e5-pawn.

There followed **7. Qe2 Qxe5 8. d4 Qxd4** (probably better is 8. . . . Qe7, followed by developing the king-knight and castling) **9. Nc3 Nf6 10. Be3 Qd8** (moving the queen for a third time) **11. O-O h6 12. Bc5** (preventing castling) **Nbd7,** arriving at Diagram 6b.

6b

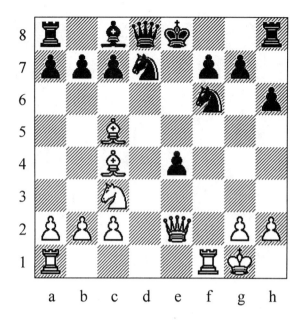

WHITE TO MOVE

Black's overambitious use of the queen was now punished by **8. Qxe4 + !! Nxe4   9. Bxf7#.**

Perhaps the most infamous misuse of the queen is the next example, Problem 6c.

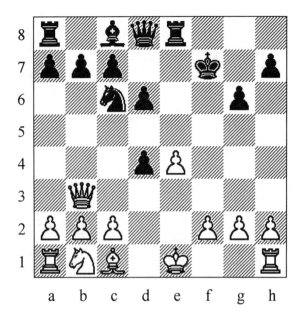

BLACK TO MOVE

This position, from the game Meek–Morphy, Mobile 1855, arose after the moves **1. e4 e5   2. Nf3 Nc6   3. d4 exd4   4. Bc4 Bc5   5. Ng5?! Nh6!   6. Nxf7? Nxf7   7. Bxf7+ Kxf7   8. Qh5+ g6   9. Qxc5 d6   10. Qb5 Re8!   11. Qb3+?.**

Attacking with a one-unit army (the queen), and without a concerted plan, White got into trouble after **11. ... d5   12. f3? Na5   13. Qd3 dxe4   14. fxe4 Qh4+   15. g3 Rxe4+   16. Kf2 Qe7   17. Nd2? Re3!   18. Qb5 c6!   19. Qf1 Bh3!   20. Qd1.**

Note that the white queen has moved eight times only to return to d1! White resigned (0–1) after **20. ... Rf8   21. Nf3 Ke8,** reaching the next diagram.

6d

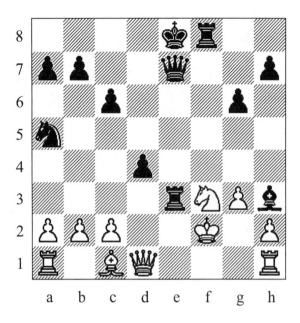

WHITE TO MOVE, RESIGNS

If 22. Bxe3, Black mates with 22. . . . Qxe3. In this final position, White's queen, two rooks, and queen-bishop occupy their original squares, while Black's cohesive pieces are poised for the kill. For White there were too many queen moves, and too much waste of time.

7

Moving the same piece several times.

In the opening you should be mobilizing your forces, moving a different piece on each turn. If, through a sequence of moves, you attack with the same piece, such as the queen, that's the only piece you'll get out. Meanwhile, your opponent can activate several units, usually gaining a significant developmental advantage. Not even a queen can do well alone against a fully armed legion.

Rx

1. Develop your minor pieces quickly in the opening.
2. Find the best square for each one.
3. When making plans, consider how all the pieces can be used.
4. If someone attacks you with just one piece, rebuff it while building your game.
5. Answer enemy threats by combining defense and counterattack, especially to the enemy king.
6. Involve as many different units as you can.

7a

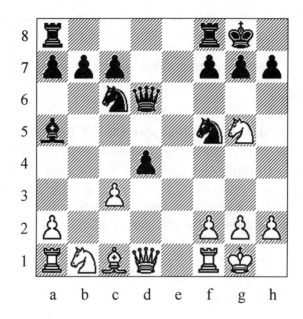

WHITE TO MOVE

This problem, from Marache–Morphy, New York 1857, was reached after **1. e4 e5   2. Nf3 Nc6   3. Bc4 Bc5   4. b4 Bxb4   5. c3 Ba5   6. d4 exd4   7. e5** (an unnecessary advance) **d5   8. exd6** (the third move for the e-pawn) **Qxd6   9. 0-0 Nge7   10. Ng5** (the second time the knight has moved) **0-0   11. Bd3** (the second move for this bishop) **Bf5   12. Bxf5 Nxf5.**

7b

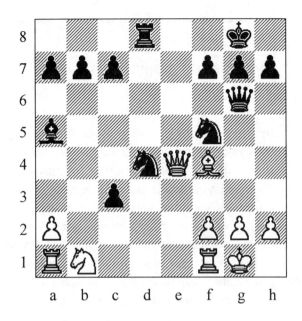

BLACK TO MOVE

White can now win the exchange, but in the process, Black builds a powerful position. Play continued: **13. Ba3 Qg6 14. Bxf8 Qxg5 15. Ba3 Rd8 16. Bc1 Qg6 17. Bf4.**

White has moved the queen-bishop five times in a row. Earlier, his king-bishop and e-pawn moved three times each, and his king-knight twice. These three units (king-bishop, king-knight, and e-pawn) are now off the board, and White has little to show for their activity.

After **17. . . . dxc3 18. Qc2 Ncd4 19. Qe4,** we reach Problem 7b. Morphy triumphed with **19. . . . Ng3!,** and White resigned in view of 20. Qxg6 Nde2#!.

In the final position, White's queen-rook and queen-knight remain undeveloped while all of Black's pieces work as a team. It's a familiar ending to a Morphy game, and it's the kind of loss one deserves after repeated moves with the same pieces.

AILMENT:

Making too many pawn moves.

In the beginning, every move is precious and has tremendous meaning. On each turn you should nurture your position, primarily by moving pieces. In this way you keep pace with your opponent and minimize weaknesses. Move a few pawns to facilitate development, of course, but if you move only or mainly pawns, the real artillery in your army never takes the field. Once your opponent's pieces penetrate your front lines, which shouldn't be too hard, you'll be at their mercy.

Rx

1. Move both center pawns fairly early to release your arsenal.
2. Advance at least one of these pawns two squares.
3. Avoid moving other pawns without clear and necessary purpose.
4. In some instances it's all right to move knight-pawns in order to develop bishops on the flank (fianchetto).
5. If you do fianchetto, be sure to develop the rest of your forces consistently with the fianchetto.
6. For example, if you move the g-pawn to flank the king-bishop, don't also move the e-pawn without a compelling reason.
7. Violate principles when necessary.
8. But don't violate them before you've learned them.

8a

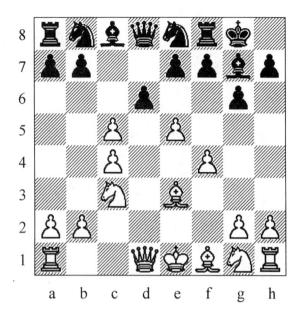

BLACK TO MOVE

White is a pawn up in this position, from Letelier–Fischer, Leipzig 1960. The opening moves were **1. d4 Nf6   2. c4 g6   3. Nc3 Bg7   4. e4 0-0   5. e5 Ne8   6. f4 d6   7. Be3 c5   8. dxc5.**

In his first eight moves White has developed only two pieces, he's not ready to castle, and his position is verging on overextension because of risky pawn advances.

The game continued: **8. . . . Nc6   9. cxd6 exd6   10. Ne4 Bf5   11. Ng3 Be6   12. Nf3 Qc7   13. Qb1 dxe5   14. f5 e4   15. fxe6 exf3   16. gxf3 f5   17. f4 Nf6   18. Be2 Rfe8   19. Kf2 Rxe6   20. Re1 Rae8   21. Bf3 Rxe3   22. Rxe3 Rxe3   23. Kxe3,** arriving at the next diagram.

8b

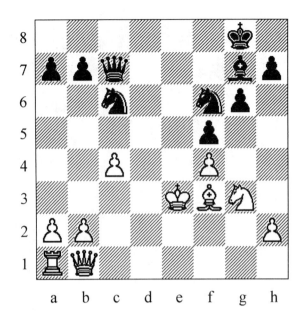

BLACK TO MOVE

White's position collapses after the brilliant **23. . . . Qxf4 + !!**, for 24. Kxf4 encounters 24. . . . Bh6 mate!

Even if White declines the queen sacrifice, he still can't save himself. For example, 25. Kf2 Ng4+ 26. Kg2 Ne3+ 27. Kf2 Nd4 28. Qh1 is met by 28. . . . Ng4+. Black's model strategy convincingly annihilated White's impetuous pawn thrusts.

8c

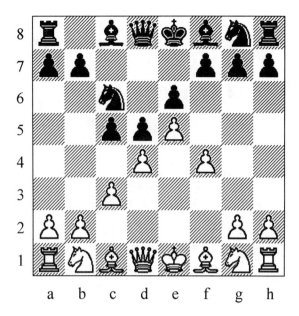

BLACK TO MOVE

This position, from the game McConnell–Morphy, New Orleans 1850, came about after **1. e4 e6   2. d4 d5   3. e5 c5   4. c3 Nc6   5. f4.**

In order to seize a spatial advantage, White started the game with five straight pawn moves. From here on he should avoid precipitating clashes until his king is safe.

The game proceeded: **5. ... Qb6   6. Nf3 Bd7   7. a3** (still another pawn move)   **7. ... Nh6** (planning to transfer this knight to f5)   **8. b4** (and another pawn move)   **8. ... cxd4   9. cxd4 Rc8   10. Bb2** (not exactly a well-placed bishop)   **10. ... Nf5   11. Qd3,** reaching Problem 8d.

8d

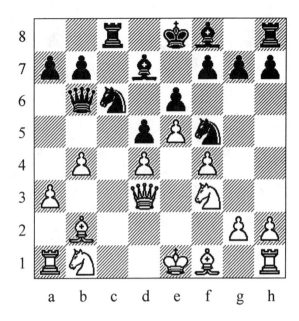

BLACK TO MOVE

White's shaky pawns and poor development now prove his undoing. Morphy broke through with **11. ... Bxb4 + ! 12. axb4 Nxb4 13. Qd2 Rc2** (the piggish rook bores in) **14. Qd1 Ne3,** and White's queen is slop.

9

Abandoning the center.

The center is the most important region of the board for both attacking and defending. Pieces placed there enjoy more scope and options. A terrific control of the center is with aligned pawns at Q4 and K4. These pawns should be backed up by other forces, especially minor pieces and rooks. If your opponent can obtain a potent pawn center and bolster it, you will have to settle for a passive position with little hope and few prospects.

Rx

1. Don't give up the center without a fight.
2. Don't relinquish it to enemy pawns unless you detect real chances to undermine your opponent's center.
3. If your opponent should establish aligned central pawns, try to force or lure them into weakening advances.
4. Drive away enemy pieces supporting the center.
5. If you can't immediately assail them, be creative and somehow find a way.
6. After destroying your opponent's center, take it with your own pieces and pawns.
7. Build up the center, using it as a base to launch attacks.
8. Don't be harried into premature attacks.

9

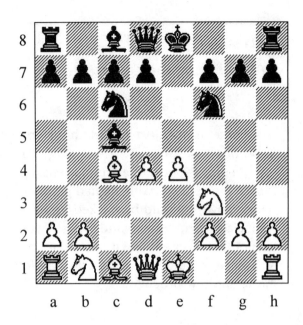

BLACK TO MOVE

In this position, achieved after the moves **1. e4 e5   2. Nf3 Nc6   3. Bc4 Bc5   4. c3 Nf6   5. d4 exd4   6. cxd4,** Black must retire his c5-bishop from attack.

The best way to do it is with a gain of time, checking on b4, when either   **7. Bd2 Bxd2 +   8. Nbxd2 d5!** or **7. Nc3 Nxe4** neutralizes White's center. But retreating the c5-bishop to b6 leaves White's center pawns unchallenged and ready to push on.

An undesirable continuation is **6. . . . Bb6?   7. d5 Ne7** (7. . . . Na5   8. Bd3 c5   9. d6! leaves Black badly constricted) **8. e5 Ng4   9. d6! cxd6   10. exd6 Nc6   11. Bg5,** and White is on top. You can't play passively when the center is at stake.

10

Developing knights to the edge.

When a knight occupies a square on an outside row, it can move to no more than four different squares. Bishops have been known to corral knights placed on the rim. Sometimes a knight doesn't do badly on the edge, especially if the center is blocked and there are no available squares. Or sometimes your tactics require a perimeter move. But usually the maxim is right: Positioning a knight on the rim is dim, if not grim.

Rx

1. Develop your knights toward the center.
2. Move them to the edge only if you must; for example, develop a knight to h3 to guard f2.
3. Practice knight shifts to useful central posts.
4. Place them on random squares and maneuver them to their destinations.
5. Determine various paths to complete the same transfers.
6. Close your eyes and try to visualize knight sequences in your mind.
7. On an empty board, time yourself moving a knight to every square. For instance, go from a1 to b1 in three moves; then from b1 to c1, etc.
8. If your opponent moves a knight to the edge, prevent it from moving back to the center.
9. Don't necessarily take it with your bishop, even though it busts up the enemy pawn structure.
10. Before taking such a knight, make sure the enemy counterplay (open knight-file, etc.) won't kill you.

10

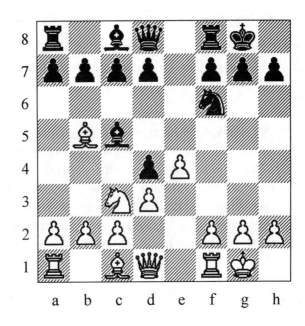

WHITE TO MOVE

In this position, which is reached after **1. e4 e5   2. Nf3 Nc6   3. Bb5 Bc5   4. Nc3 Nf6   5. 0-0 0-0   6. d3 Nd4   7. Nxd4 exd4,** Black's d4-pawn pricks White's c3-knight.

White could simply retreat the knight to e2, though he might be lured into playing **8. Na4?** because of the attack to the c5-bishop.

But after **8. . . . Be7,** White has to address the threat of 9. . . . c6 followed by 10. . . . b5, forcing the b5-bishop and a4-knight to stumble over each other in frantic flight.

11

AILMENT:

Developing knights only to the second rank.

At full mobility, a knight has access to exactly eight squares. This is true when a knight is on any of bishop-three squares (f3, c3, f6, and c6), which are ideal places to develop knights in the opening. Less good are the king-two (e2 and e7) and queen-two (d2 and d7) squares, which offer a knight no more than six places, and the rook-three squares, which offer only four.

Rx

1. Aim to develop your knights to the third rank.
2. Move them toward the center, especially to the bishop-three squares.
3. Don't put them on the edge without a specific reason.
4. Be sure of yourself before developing them to the second rank.
5. If your opponent puts his knights on the second rank, move in on the squares they leave vulnerable.
6. For example, a white knight placed on e2 doesn't guard h4, allowing Black's queen the possibility of invading there.
7. Stop the opposing queen from going to your KR4 by developing your KN to KB3.
8. If your opponent's king-knight sits on the second rank, look to fuel a kingside attack.
9. Judge every situation in context.

11a

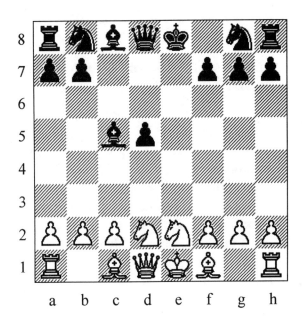

BLACK TO MOVE

This position arises after **1. e4 e6   2. d4 d5   3. Nd2 c5   4. exd5 exd5   5. dxc5 Bxc5   6. Ne2?.**

White's knights are a total encumbrance to central development. Indeed, after **6. ...Qb6,** White's lack of fluidity renders defense of f2 difficult.

One of the awkward knights must go, for 7. Nf3 Bxf2+   8. Kd2 Qe3# and 7. Nc3 Bxf2+   8. Ke2 Qe3# end in the same joke mate.

11b

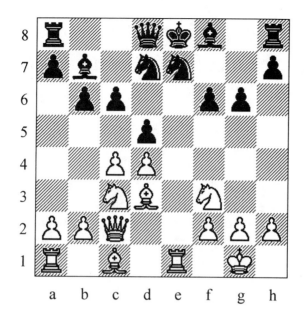

WHITE TO MOVE

Play out **1. d4 d5   2. c4 e6   3. Nc3 Ne7?   4. Nf3 Nd7?** (look at the scopeless black knights) **5. Qc2 c6   e4 f6?   7. Bd3 g6** (White was indirectly threatening Black's h-pawn) **8. 0-0 b6   9. Re1** (setting up a potential pin on the e-file) **9. . . . Bb7   10. exd5 exd5** and you have Problem 11b.

Black's passive knights and inoperative bishops are no help against **11. Bxg6 + ! hxg6   12. Qxg6#**. Let's face it: Knights often don't do well on the second rank.

12 | AILMENT:
Bringing the queen to an assailable center square.

The queen is super-radiant from the center, but the chances are small of safely establishing it there in the opening. If attacked by pawns, knights, or bishops (very real possibilities), you'll have to waste time moving it to balmier climes. Your opponent will benefit by being able to develop at your expense, if it doesn't cost you in more material ways as well.

Rx

1. Don't bring the queen to the middle in the beginning, unless clearly worthwhile or needed.
2. Rely instead on your minor pieces and pawns.
3. Don't embark on plans that might force the queen to the center.
4. If your queen is already in the center, or can't help going there, watch out for ambushes.
5. Be prepared to transfer the queen to a risk-free environment, preferably with a gain of time.
6. It helps to hide your king, reducing the chance of double attacks to king and queen.
7. Don't be general when you must be specific.

12

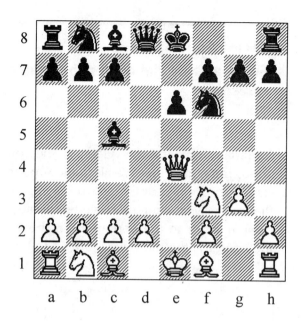

WHITE TO MOVE

This diagram is based on the moves **1. e4 e6   2. Qe2 Bc5   3. g3 d5   4. Nf3 dxe4   5. Qxe4 Nf6.**

Black has gained a free developing move for his king-knight by attacking White's queen, which now must move to safety. Instead of retiring the queen from the center, however, White tries to keep it there with **6. Qe5?,** perhaps figuring to gain time by hitting the c5-bishop.

But Black imposes a penalty for this brashness with **6. ... Bxf2 + !,** when **7. Kxf2** would be stoned by a forking knight check on g4. So White must move his king to safety, ceding the right to castle, and Black's bishop escapes with a free pawn. So much for compulsive queen moves in the center.

13

AILMENT:

Surrendering the center to the enemy queen.

Generally, bringing the queen to the center is not good, but sometimes it's all right. Suppose circumstances prevent your queen from being attacked, or the only ways the queen could be threatened would bring disaster to the opponent. In those instances, the center is the place for a queen to be.

Rx

1. Don't automatically trade pieces so the enemy queen comes to the center.
2. If you're thinking of bringing the enemy queen to the center, make sure that you can then drive it away usefully, without debilitating your position.
3. If your opponent's queen is already established there, try to attack it productively with pawns and/or minor pieces.
4. Consider the possibility of forcing a queen trade.
5. In endings especially, don't cede the center to the enemy queen.

13a

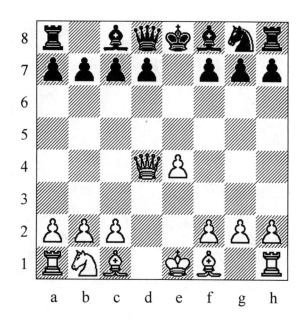

BLACK TO MOVE

Problem 13a is created by the moves **1. e4 e5   2. Nf3 Nc6   3. d4 exd4   4. Nxd4 Nxd4?   5. Qxd4.**

White's queen incandesces from the center, thanks to Black's poor decision to trade knights. Since the only way to attack the queen, c7-c5, causes permanent weaknesses in Black's position (check out d5 and d6, for starters), Black must tolerate the central placement of White's dominant piece.

13b

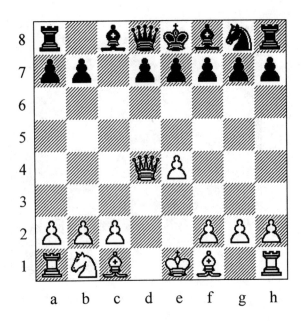

BLACK TO MOVE

The same kind of egregious exchange can take place in the Sicilian Defense, as in **1. e4 c5   2. Nf3 Nc6   3. d4 cxd4   4. Nxd4 Nxd4?   5. Qxd4.** Here, too, White's queen has a once-a-year day.

14

Missing a fork trick.

Even if a tactic doesn't win material, it still can lead to a superior position or an improvement of your situation. The fork trick (temporarily sacrificing a knight for an enemy center pawn because the piece can be gotten back by a follow-up pawn fork) destroys the opponent's center, and it may also discombobulate the enemy forces. Too often we miss seeing that we can do this to our opponent, or that it can be done to us.

Usually, if you're inflicting it on your opponent, the main drawback is that he might be able to countersacrifice his bishop on your KB2, possibly preventing castling, though this is often a reasonable price to pay for blowing out the enemy center.

Rx

1. If your opponent has aligned center pawns, see if you can play a fork trick.
2. Especially try to do this if you are castled and your opponent isn't.
3. Before playing a fork trick, determine if your opponent has a countersacrifice on your KB2.
4. If so, determine if you can castle by hand afterward.
5. Especially look out for enemy knights checking on your KN4.
6. If you're already castled, his countersacrifice should have no bite.

7. If you have a pair of center pawns abreast on your fourth rank, discourage the fork trick being used against you.
8. You probably can avoid it by retreating your bishop from QB4 to QN3.
9. Another way to dissuade it is to overprotect your e-pawn.

14a

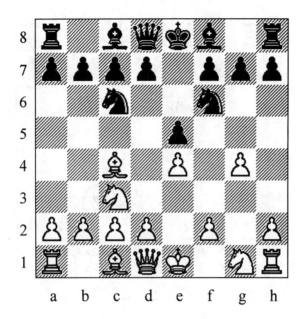

BLACK TO MOVE

This position, reached after **1. e4 e5 2. Nc3 Nf6 3. Bc4 Nc6 4. g4**, is an example of a misguided attempt by White to commence wing activity early in the game. Usually the best counter to a flank attack is to strike in the center.

The fork trick **4. ... Nxe4! 5. Nxe4 d5** regains the piece, destroys White's center, and leaves the g4-pawn weak and looking silly. White could have avoided this fork trick by the commonsense **4. d3**, solidifying the e-pawn.

14b

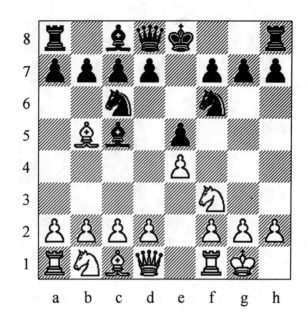

8

7

6

5

4

3

2

1

a b c d e f g h

WHITE TO MOVE

Many openings rely on fork tricks to neutralize the enemy center and create confusion. Problem 14b shows such a variation from the Ruy Lopez: **1. e4 e5   2. Nf3 Nc6   3. Bb5 Nf6   4. 0-0 Bc5.** White wreaks havoc with **5. Nxe5! Nxe5   6. d4,** and the attack proceeds apace, as Black's pieces collide with each other.

14c

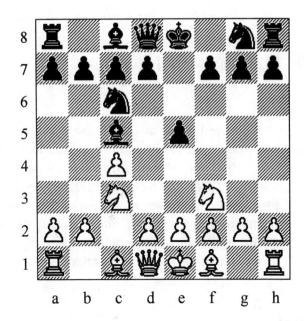

It doesn't have to be a double king-pawn opening to provide a fork trick, as in the case of the English Opening's **1. c4 e5   2. Nc3 Nc6   3. Nf3 Bc5.**

The real culprit is **3. . . . Bc5**, allowing **4. Nxe5!**. White gets the piece back no matter what. If 4. . . . Nxe5, then 5. d4; or if 4. . . . Bxf2+, then 5. Kxf2 Nxe5   6. e4, with good activity in the center for the loss of castling. A timely fork trick can gain a central advantage.

15

AILMENT:
Letting the initiative slip.

If you have the initiative you can control the flow of play. Lose it and this ability passes to your opponent. How does it happen? In several ways: You play without a plan, or make unessential moves, or neglect your development, or expend too much time trying to win irrelevant material. But do the right things and your opponent should be on the defensive for as long as you're in charge.

Rx

1. Maintain the initiative by combining attack with development.
2. Let it dissipate at your own peril.
3. Don't waste moves; each one should count.
4. With each move, try to develop a new piece and attack enemy targets.
5. If your opponent has the initiative, look for opportunities to seize it.
6. Thwart threats by merging defense with counterattack.
7. Don't trade pieces when you have the initiative.
8. If your opponent has the initiative, swap off his peskiest invaders.

15

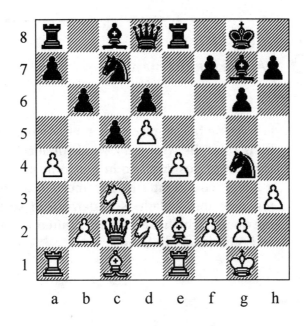

This position comes from the game Gurgenidze–Tal, USSR 1958. The opening moves were **1. d4 Nf6   2. c4 c5   3. d5 e6   4. Nc3 exd5   5. cxd5 d6   6. Nf3 g6   7. e4 Bg7   8. Be2 0-0   9. 0-0 Re8   10. Nd2 Na6   11. Re1 Nc7   12. a4 b6   13. Qc2 Ng4   14. h3?.**

To maintain a slight pull, White should have played 14. Bxg4, and followed 14. . . . Bxg4 by 15. Nc4. Tal now stole the initiative and won brilliantly.

Play continued: **14. . . . Nxf2!   15. Kxf2 Qh4+   16. Kf1 Bd4   17. Nd1 Qxh3!   18. Bf3 Qh2   19. Ne3 f5   20. Ndc4 fxe4   21. Bxe4 Ba6   22. Bf3 Re5   23. Ra3 Rae8   24. Bd2 Nxd5   25. Bxd5+ Rxd5   26. Ke2 Bxe3   27. Rxe3 Bxc4+** and Black won. If 28. Qxc4, then 28. . . . Qxg2+   29. Kd1 Qxd2 is mate. It doesn't take much to purloin the initiative.

16

AILMENT:
Attacking prematurely.

Everything has its place and time. Attack the wrong thing or at the wrong time and you'll achieve nothing, out of position and in sad confusion, prone to a killing counterattack. The most frequent occurrence of this malady is undercooked sorties with the queen, which are usually rebuffed by computers and other sentient beings.

Rx

1. Don't begin an attack unless your forces are developed adequately.
2. Arm yourself with the proper backup firepower.
3. Try to attack with a number of pieces, not just one or two.
4. Don't begin every analysis by "reaching" for the queen.
5. When you analyze, shift perspective.
6. Pretend you are your opponent, trying to answer your own threats.
7. If you can answer your own attacks, don't play them.
8. Resist making unsupportable pawn attacks.
9. Don't advance without having a definite target.
10. Do the right thing, but do it at the right time.

16

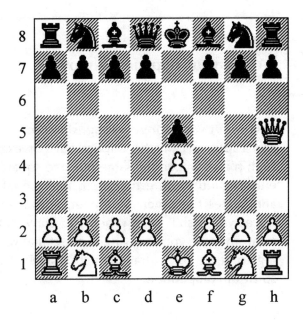

BLACK TO MOVE

I've been revulsed by this position, created by **1. e4 e5   2. Qh5,** countless times in my classes and at tournaments.

Undoubtedly because of a fascination with the queen's muscle, inexperienced players resort to this sudden attack, hitting the e-pawn and preparing to play Bf1-c4, hoping for a Scholar's Mate (Qh5xf7).

It shouldn't work, though, because Black hasn't done anything wrong. Indeed, after **2. . . . Nc6   3. Bc4 g6** (or even 3. . . . Qe7 followed by 4. . . . Nf6) **4. Qf3 Nf6,** White isn't better developed than Black.

If White pushes the assault further with **5. Qb3?,** he must contend with **5. . . . Nd4,** when 6. Bxf7+ Ke7   7. Qc4 b5 actually gains the f7-bishop.

A 1956 game, NN–Albertson, continued **6. Qd3 d5   7. Bxd5? Nxd5   8. exd5 Bf5   9. Qg3 Nxc2+   10. Kd1 Nxa1   11. Qxe5+ Qe7   12. Qxh8 Bc2#.** Cool heads should prevail over frenzied assailants. Be sure your attacks are justified.

17

AILMENT:
Aping your opponent's moves.

This won't work for very long, since certain checks and captures can't be duplicated. For example, if both players move the same piece to squares where either could capture the other, the one taking first annihilates the other. Moreover, if your opponent mates you it's all over. When you copy your opponent's moves, you're saying in effect that you're willing to settle for a draw, which is against the very spirit of competition.

Rx

1. Don't imitate your opponent's play without just cause.
2. Look for creative ways to break symmetry.
3. Especially find moves that take the initiative, such as threats, checks, or captures.
4. Disguise your intentions and give false signals.
5. Trick your opponent into thinking you're copying him, then surprise him with a twist.
6. Play over games with symmetrical lines and see how masters infuse such positions with character.
7. Go first, unless it's better to go second!

17

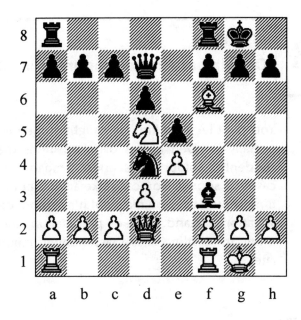

WHITE TO MOVE

This symmetrical position is arrived at after **1. e4 e5   2. Nf3 Nc6   3. Nc3 Nf6   4. Bb5 Bb4   5. 0-0 0-0   6. d3 d6   7. Bg5 Bg4   8. Nd5 Nd4   9. Nxb4 Nxb5   10. Nd5 Nd4   11. Bxf6 Bxf3   12. Qd2 Qd7** (Problem 17).

In this slapdash variation, Black has mindlessly aped White for twelve moves, but the mirror image can be broken by the checking **13. Ne7+.** In order to stop mate (13. . . . Kh8   14. Bxg7+ Kxg7   15. Qg5+ Kh8   16. Qf6#), Black must give up his queen for the meddlesome knight. The copying ends here, as it often does, with the defeat of the second player.

18 AILMENT:
Delaying castling or not preparing it.

You can't let your king be caught in the middle, especially in open games or in positions that might suddenly explode. This doesn't mean you should castle as soon as you can. Like any other move, castling should only be played if it's a good idea in the situation at hand. It takes preparation, though. To prime for castling at the last moment might be too late.

Rx

1. Ready yourself for castling early in the game.
2. At least on the wing in which you intend to castle, develop both minor pieces.
3. Avoid potential weaknesses in the anticipated castled position.
4. Refrain from moving the pawns on that side.
5. Don't allow the middle to open with your king still in it.
6. Don't expose key lines and squares so that your opponent could prevent you from castling.
7. Be especially careful if the opening is unfamiliar.
8. Arrange practice contests where your chief aim is to castle within eight moves.
9. Don't rely on the rules, because every situation has its own rules.

18

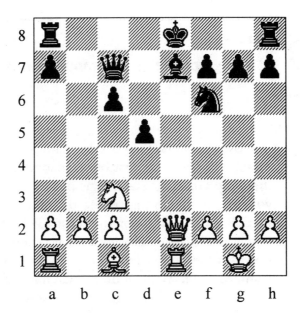

BLACK TO MOVE

White is doubly attacking the e7-bishop, and it appears Black can't castle without abandoning it. But surprisingly, 1. . . . 0-0! works, for 2. Qxe7 is met by a black rook move to e8, forcing White to give up his queen.

Instead, Black played 1. . . . Rb8?, which crashed against 2. Bf4!, when 2. . . . Qxf4 is answered by 3. Qxe7#. Delaying castling cost Black a rook.

19

Letting your king get trapped in the center.

In most openings, the center is a hotbed of activity. Attacks, threats, and possible exchanges can happen there right from the start. If the position opens while your king is still in the center, it could become vulnerable. Even if your opponent can't get at your king immediately, he might be able to keep it pinned down in the center indefinitely by preventing you from castling. With your monarch exposed, and with nowhere to hide, the end is likely near.

Rx

1. Never lose sight of the center.
2. Don't let the center open if you're uncastled.
3. Don't open the center when behind in development.
4. Don't engage in transactions that could expose your king.
5. Castle before commencing any activity that could lead to line-opening central exchanges.
6. Be alert to enemy pieces getting into position to prevent you from castling.
7. If enemy pieces are so placed, block them, drive them away, or destroy them.
8. In difficult situations, make practical decisions.

19

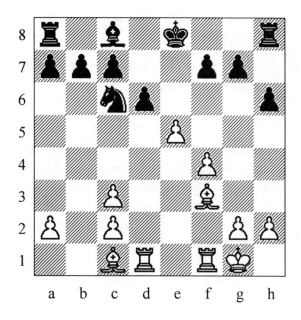

BLACK TO MOVE

Black's position, from the game Pandolfini–Morrison, New York 1964, is under extreme pressure. His king is still in the center, and White's pieces are perched for raw aggression.

Meanwhile, Black's d-pawn looks like a goner. Probably best is castling kingside, or developing the queen-bishop and castling queenside, accepting the loss of a pawn.

But Black continued **1. . . . dxe5?**, which led to **2. Ba3!**, trapping Black's king in the center. To make matters worse, there followed **2. . . . exf4? 3. Rfe1 + Be6 4. Rxe6 + ! fxe6 5. Bh5 +**, with mate next move. Black's king was caught in the crossfire of the two bishops.

20

AILMENT:

Allowing a check that takes away your right to castle.

If the center opens with your king still there, a check could be particularly annoying. You might have to block the check, submitting to an unpleasant pin, or worse, move your king, forfeiting the castling privilege. Once that happens, you're at the mercy of the oncoming horde.

Rx

1. Before you allow the center to open, make sure your king is secure.
2. Get ready for attack by castling.
3. When circumstances require you to pursue central activity with your king on its original square, carefully consider the war zone.
4. Not all checks are meaningful, so try to determine if your opponent has potentially dangerous ones.
5. If you must move your king, castle by hand (move the rook out of the corner and retreat the king to safety).
6. Try to prevent your opponent from castling.
7. Pursue your plans while frustrating your opponent's.

20a

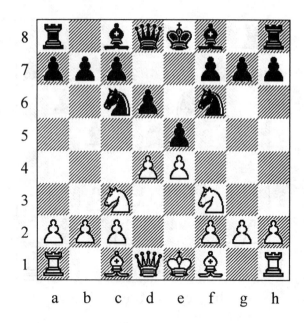

WHITE TO MOVE

Problem 20a occurs after **1. e4 e5   2. Nf3 Nc6   3. Nc3 Nf6   4. d4 d6?.**.

Black's last move, d7-d6, protects the e-pawn but leads to problems. It allows White, by forceful exchanges, to insure that Black's king will remain stuck in the center, subject to troublesome attacks.

In the game Joyce–Ross, New York 1977, play continued **5. dxe5 Nxe5   6. Nxe5 dxe5   7. Qxd8+** (trading queens to deprive Black of the castling privilege) **Kxd8.**

With a pressing initiative, White was able to pilfer a pawn: **8. Bg5 Bb4   9. Bxf6+** (doubling Black's pawns and fixing f7 as a target) **gxf6   10. 0-0-0+ Bd7** (blocking the check, but putting the bishop in an uncomfortable pin)   **11. Nd5 Be7   12. Bc4 Rg8   13. g3 c6   14. Nxe7 Kxe7   15. Bxf7.** In this game, losing the ability to castle was a big problem.

20b

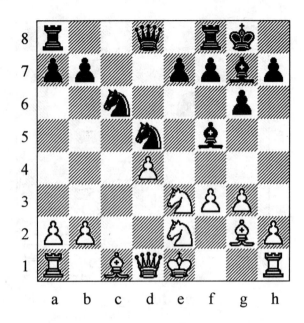

BLACK TO MOVE

Problem 20b is from the game Potemkin–Alekhine, St. Petersburg 1912. The preceding moves were **1. e4 c5   2. g3 g6   3. Bg2 Bg7   4. Ne2 Nc6   5. c3 Nf6   6. Na3 d5   7. exd5 Nxd5   8. Nc2 0-0   9. d4 cxd4   10. cxd4 Bg4   11. f3 Bf5   12. Ne3?.**

White's last move was a mistake. He should have used the tempo to castle. Now Black took away the castling privilege with **12. ... Qa5 + !**, because 13. Bd2 is answered by 13. . . . Nxe3!.

Forced to move his king, White soon succumbed after **13. Kf2 Ndb4   14. Nxf5 Qxf5   15. g4 Nd3 +   16. Kg3** (16. Kf1 Qb5) **Nxd4   17. gxf5 Nxf5 +   18. Kg4 h5 +   19. Kh3 Nf2#.**

21

Moving rook to queen-one instead of castling queenside.

It's so easy to make this mistake. You see a useful developing move of the queen-rook to queen-one and do it without another thought. You thereby miss the possibility of killing two birds with one stone by castling queenside. This also puts the queen-rook on queen-one, but, even better, it gets your king to safety for the same money.

Rx

1. Whenever you have the option of castling queenside, consider it.
2. Don't castle queenside if it endangers your king.
3. Castle queenside if it's safe and saves time.
4. Castle queenside if you're contemplating a kingside pawn storm.
5. If castling queenside seems risky but you need a rook on queen-one, move the rook.
6. Don't base your analysis on superficial concerns.
7. In practice games, castle queenside when reasonable to learn how to play those positions.

21

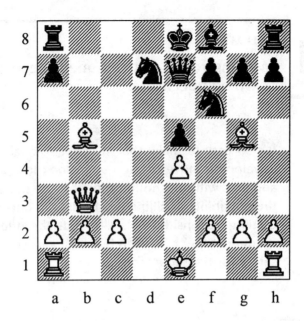

WHITE TO MOVE

Problem 21 comes from a famous game between Paul Morphy and an amateur team of two aristocrats, played in Paris in 1858. The opening moves were **1. e4 e5   2. Nf3 d6   3. d4 Bg4?   4. dxe5 Bxf3   5. Qxf3 dxe5   6. Bc4 Nf6   7. Qb3 Qe7   8. Nc3 c6   9. Bg5 b5   10. Nxb5! cxb5   11. Bxb5+ Nbd7.**

White wants to put more pressure on the pinned black knight at d7, so he immediately considers Ra1-d1. But by castling queen-side instead, White's rook moves to d1 while at the same time his king reaches safety and unclogs the home rank to connect the rooks.

The game sped on to its exciting conclusion with **12. 0-0-0 Rd8   13. Rxd7 Rxd7   14. Rd1** (it's a good thing White's king is out of the way) **Qe6   15. Bxd7+ Nxd7   16. Qb8+ Nxb8   17. Rd8#.** In the end, the king-rook did the job because White castled queenside!

22

AILMENT:

Castling into danger.

Most of the time, you castle to connect your rooks and get your king to safety. But suppose by castling you actually transfer your king to an exposed wing where enemy pieces are poised for the kill. When castling on a particular side seems precarious, it's better to castle in the other direction or not at all.

Rx

1. Castling should never be considered a sine qua non.
2. Before you castle, check where the king is headed.
3. Don't castle if your pawns on that side have been moved and are weak.
4. Don't castle on the side where the enemy has potential targets and open lines.
5. Don't castle on the side where enemy pawns seem poised for an avalanche.
6. Don't castle there if enemy pieces seem aimed and loaded.
7. If your opponent castles on such a vulnerable side, throw everything into the attack against his king.
8. Odds are such assault tactics will work.

22

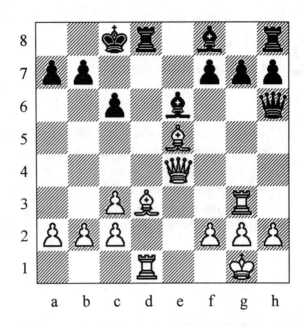

WHITE TO MOVE

This is from the game Lasker–Englund, Scheveningen 1913. The starting moves were **1. e4 e5   2. Nf3 Nc6   3. Nc3 Nf6   4. Bb5 Nd4   5. Nxe5 Qe7   6. Nf3 Nxe4?   7. 0-0 Nxc3   8. dxc3 Nxf3+   9. Qxf3 Qc5   10. Re1+ Be7   11. Bd3 d5   12. Be3 Qd6   13. Bf4 Qf6   14. Qxd5! c6   15. Qe4 Be6   16. Re3 Bc5   17. Be5 Qh6   18. Rg3 Bf8   19. Rd1.**

White's last move contains a subtle trap. If Black plays thoughtlessly and castles queenside, he gets mated. That's exactly what happened: **19. . . . 0-0-0?** (Problem 22) **20. Qxc6+! bxc6   21. Ba6#.** No, castling isn't always a good move.

AILMENT:

Castling on the wrong side.

This occurs when you are able to castle on either side but choose the wrong one. Mistakes of this nature can be offensive or defensive. Offensive castling errors usually involve castling on the same side as your opponent. You'd like to launch a full-scale attack against his king, but the presence of your own king on the same side requires you to act with caution. Defensive errors usually concern castling into danger instead of on the other side, where it's safer.

Rx

1. Before castling, decide on which side your king will be safest.
2. Determine also whether you have real chances of pawn-storming your opponent's king.
3. If you castle, head in the most dependable direction.
4. Make sure the enemy pieces there are not dangerous.
5. If your opponent castles first, castle the other way before pursuing a pawn storm.
6. When feasible, delay castling until your opponent has tipped his hand, but don't delay beyond reason.
7. To cultivate your attacking skills, play practice games where you agree to castle on opposite sides to get experience with pawn storms.

23

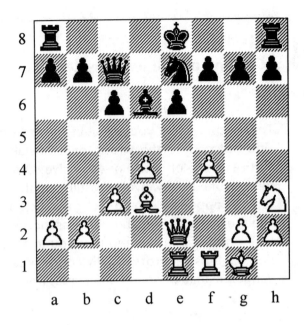

BLACK TO MOVE

White has developed all his pieces and has mounted pressure in the center. The time has come for Black to castle, but on which side? The correct move is 1. . . . . 0-0-0, heading queenside.

The other way is definitely the wrong one, for **1. . . . 0-0?** allows a classic bishop sacrifice, **2. Bxh7 + !,** when **2. . . . Kxh7   3. Qh5 +** is troubling.

For example, 3. . . . Kg8 goes down to 4. Ng5 Re8   5. Qxf7 +, followed by a rook lift to the third rank or even Ng5xe6. In this case, castling kingside is tantamount to castling in the sand.

24

AILMENT:

Castling and losing a pawn.

It's easy to overlook and drop a pawn, if not worse. When your king is in the center and your queen-rook is unmoved, QR2 and KB2 are guarded: QR2 by the rook, and KB2 by the king. But once you castle queenside, neither points are held up by their original defenses. So if these squares are attacked before castling, they're particularly vulnerable after castling. Captures of pawns on these squares could very well be demolishing. Imagine White's shock, castled queenside, suddenly seeing Black's queen swoop down on a2.

Rx

1. Before castling queenside, take one last look at two points: QR2 and KB2.
2. If they are already under attack, don't castle without weighing the consequences.
3. Determine if you can allow the enemy to capture or invade on those squares.
4. If you can't, castle kingside if it seems good.
5. Or take steps to safeguard these potential targets so that you can then castle queenside afterward.
6. If your opponent is about to castle queenside, take aim at his QR2 and/or KB2.
7. Do this several moves before your opponent castles queenside and he might overlook the danger.

24

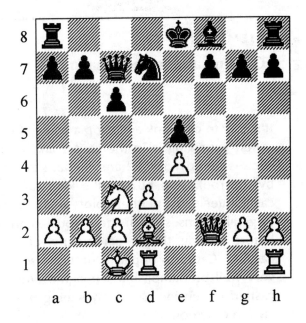

BLACK TO MOVE

In this quiet-looking position, Black should proceed with caution. He could develop his bishop to c5, gaining time by attacking White's queen, but then he has to have a good answer to Qf2-g3, attacking g7. If Black were to castle kingside at that point, Bd2-h6 would prove embarrassing.

But castling queenside in the diagram position wouldn't work either, for White's queen could safely capture Black's a-pawn or f-pawn, both of which would be left undefended. Possibly Black should try 1. . . . . Nc5, with the idea of putting the knight on e6.

25

AILMENT:

Castling into a pin.

This disease occurs along the diagonals leading to the king after castling. If you castle kingside and the f-pawn is no longer on its original square, for example, you could be vulnerable along the QR7-KN1 diagonal. If you castle queenside, the soft line is the QB1-KR6 diagonal. If on the same line you have a potentially susceptible piece, such as the queen, a bishop pin could start an ulcer.

Rx

1. Before castling kingside, examine the diagonal leading to KN1.
2. If the f-pawn is out of place, determine if any of your pieces are in position to be pinned.
3. Don't think you're safe just because you were safe on the previous move.
4. Look further to see if your opponent has line-clearing, time-gaining advances.
5. Make a similar check for the QB1-KR6 diagonal before castling queenside.
6. Especially look out for the enemy queen and king-bishop.

25

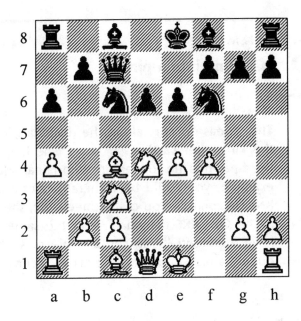

WHITE TO MOVE

Problem 25 comes from a variation of the Sicilian Defense: **1. e4 c5   2. Nf3 Nc6   3. d4 cxd4   4. Nxd4 e6   5. Nc3 a6   6. a4 Nf6   7. f4 d6   8. Bc4 Qc7.**

White should be concerned about potential discoveries to his king-bishop along the c-file, but he might be tranquilized into thinking he's covered, for Nc6xd4 seems answerable by Qd1xd4, guarding the c4-bishop.

Yet if White castles, **9. 0-0?,** Black wins at least a piece by **10. ... Nxd4,** for **11. Qxd4** meets up with **11. ... d5!**. Suddenly, White must save his bishop as well as ward off the coming Bf8-c5, pinning the queen.

26

AILMENT:
Castling into a skewer.

Here you get your king to safety by castling, but your opponent's queen-bishop skewers your queen and castled rook. If you castle kingside, the danger arises along the QR6-KB1 diagonal, and if you castle queenside, you get it along the Q1-KR5 diagonal.

Rx

1. Be careful about castling kingside when your queen occupies the QR6-KB1 diagonal.
2. Determine if the enemy queen-bishop can skewer your queen and rook after castling.
3. If you castle kingside, especially look out for the enemy queen-bishop going to its QR3.
4. If you castle queenside, watch out for the enemy queen-bishop moving to your KN4.
5. Try to sense these dangers before castling.
6. Imagine you are your opponent.

26a

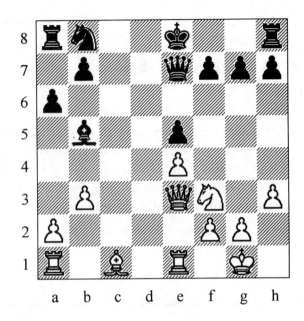

BLACK TO MOVE

White has the better of it here, with slightly superior development, fewer weaknesses, and greater attacking chances. If there's a muddying factor it's the opposite-color bishops, which provide some hope for a draw.

But Black should step carefully, for the logical move, castling kingside, **1. . . . 0-0?,** is cut down by **2. a4.** After Black retreats his bishop, White skewers queen and castled king-rook by Bc1-a3.

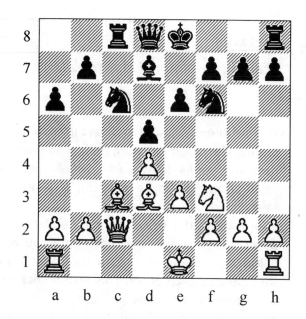

WHITE TO MOVE

This position poses a more complicated version of the same idea. White appears to be all right, in that his back rank is clear of queen and minor pieces and he's ready to castle. Since castling queenside seems to place the king in the direction of Black's attack, White chooses to castle kingside, **1. 0-0?**

Unfortunately, this runs into a losing exchange of minor pieces, **1. . . . Nb4** (safe because of the pin on the c-file) **2. Qd2 Nxd3   3. Qxd3.** And now, with White's queen on the same diagonal as his newly castled king-rook, Black gains the exchange by the skewer **3. . . . Bb5.**

27

AILMENT:

Failing to connect the rooks.

This problem is linked to delays in castling and completing development. Generally, you'll want to connect the rooks fairly early, which means quickly castling and getting everything else off the home rank.

Although the queen functions like a rook, you don't really connect the rooks until you've also developed your queen. When rooks are connected, they defend each other. This means that either one can move to an open file and, if captured by an enemy rook, be replaced by its partner, maintaining a presence on the file.

Rx

1. In order to connect the rooks, mobilize all four of your minor pieces quickly.
2. Castle.
3. Develop the queen.
4. If you can't do all this in time, be cautious about seizing open files when the enemy's rook can oppose you.
5. In that case, you may have to surrender control of the file.
6. When studying an opening, make sure you know when and how the rooks generally connect.
7. In your practice, try to play games in which you connect your rooks within the first twelve moves.

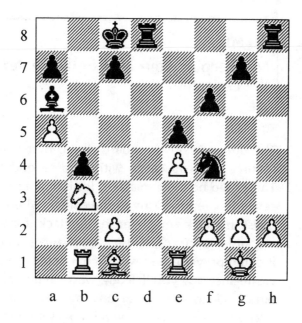

WHITE TO MOVE

White is already castled, but since his queen-bishop remains undeveloped, his rooks don't defend each other (they're not connected). The best move for White is the simple capture, 1. Bxf4, solving the home rank problem and ridding the position of Black's carnivorous knight.

But being offensively minded, White neglects to prepare properly and instead invades, **1. Nc5?,** tormenting the a6-bishop but keeping his rooks unjoined.

There follows 1. . . . Ne2+, when 2. Kf1 Nc3+ gains at least the exchange. Since 2. Rxe2 leads to a back-rank mate for Black, White tries **2. Kh1?,** which ends in mate by **2. . . . Rxh2+! 3. Kxh2 Rh8+ 4. Bh6 Rxh6#.** Punishment can be swift when you fail to connect your rooks.

28

The queen is off the board, the center is relatively secure, and you castle without a second thought. This could be a big mistake, for it might make more sense to keep the king in the center, where it could assist in attack and defense. In attack, for example, it could support certain pawn advances. In defense, it could prevent the invasion of enemy rooks. If you castle instead, you'll likely waste time carting the king back to the center anyhow. You simply can't afford to throw away several moves so heedlessly.

Rx

1. Once you've reached the endgame, don't automatically castle.
2. Determine if it's necessary to castle at all.
3. Might it not be better to stay in the center?
4. In the endgame, the king should be used as a weapon.
5. Try to activate your king before your opponent activates his.
6. Familiarize yourself with middlegames and endgames typically arising from your openings.
7. Free yourself from stereotypical thinking. You don't always have to castle.

28a

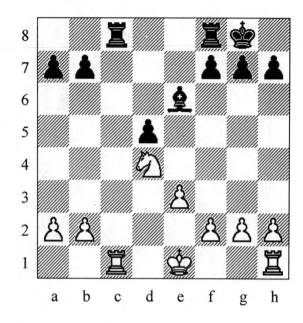

WHITE TO MOVE

White's c1-rook is menaced. White can exchange rooks, 1. Rxc8 Rxc8, but that gives Black temporary control of the c-file. Or he can connect his rooks by castling kingside, which is certainly plausible.

Or, if he has a bent for the endgame, he might simply keep his king in the center with 1. Kd2. This connects the rooks, adds protection to c1, and prepares the king for activity in the center and on the queenside once the rooks come off. On d2 the king is actually quite safe, shielded from rook attack on the d-file and occupying a dark square that is unassailable by the enemy bishop.

28b

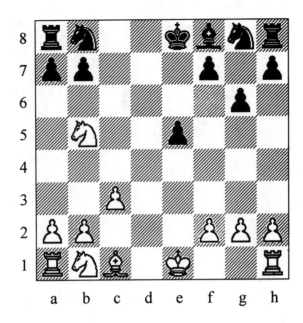

BLACK TO MOVE

The game Merenyi–Capablanca, Budapest 1928, reached this position after **1. e4 c5   2. Nf3 g6   3. c3 d5   4. Bb5+ Bd7   5. Bxd7+ Qxd7   6. exd5 Qxd5   7. d4 cxd4   8. Qxd4 Qxd4   9. Nxd4 e5   10. Nb5.**

At first glance, Black seems to be pressed, for the intrusive white knight aims at c7. Capablanca opted not to play 10. . . . Na6, but instead went with the bold **10. . . . Kd7!,** immediately involving his king in the fray. White then followed suit, keeping his king in the center also with **11. Ke2** (see Problem 28c).

28c

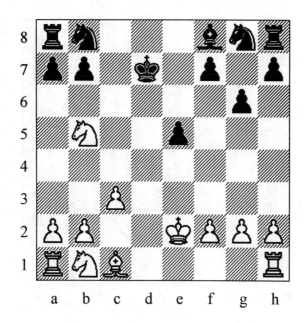

BLACK TO MOVE

Capablanca now played **11. . . . Kc6!**, repositioning his king so that he could smoothly coordinate the rest of his forces.

Play continued: **12. a4 Nd7   13. Be3 a6   14. Rd1 Ngf6   15. Nd2 Rd8   16. Na3 Nd5   17. Ndc4 b6   18. Rd2 Bxa3   19. Rxa3 Rhe8   20. Nd6 Re7   21. c4 Nxe3   22. fxe3 Nc5   23. Ne4 Rxd2+   24. Nxd2 a5   25. Nb1 Rd7   26. Nd2 e4   27. Nb3 Nd3   28. Nd4+ Kc5   29. b3 f5   30. Ra1** (see Problem 28d).

28d

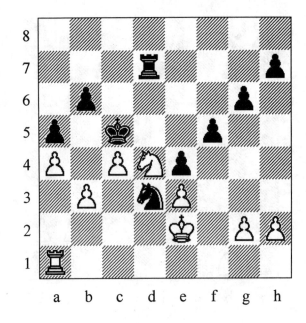

BLACK TO MOVE

Black's king is beautifully stationed for the final break-through. The game concluded: **30. . . . Rxd4! 31. exd4+ Kxd4** (what terrific king placement) **32. g3 g5** (here come the pawns) **33. b4 f4 34. c5 f3+ 35. Kf1 e3 36. Re1 bxc5 37. Rxe3 Kxe3 38. bxa5 c4,** and White resigned. A likely end is 39. a6 c3 40. a7 c2 41. a8/Q c1/Q#.

29

Moving the f-pawn unwisely.

Moving the f-pawn typically has either or both of two functions: to exert pressure against the enemy e-pawn or to open the f-file. The latter is particularly applicable when you've castled kingside. Exchanging off the f-pawn gives your castled rook a clear route to the opponent's camp. Even when you don't exchange off the f-pawn, the rook might still be able to move to the third rank on the f-file to shift over for attack. But pushing the f-pawn early can have the drawback of exposing your king to pesky queen checks along the weakened K1-KR4 diagonal.

Rx

1. Don't move the f-pawn without careful consideration.
2. If uncastled, can you move it and survive a queen check at your KR4?
3. Can the enemy queen then shift from your KR4 to your K4 with check?
4. If castled kingside, will moving the f-pawn expose you to checks along your QR7-KN1 diagonal?
5. Especially watch out for forking queen checks.
6. Never play a double-edged move without considering how it could falter.
7. Before playing it, give it one final look.

29a

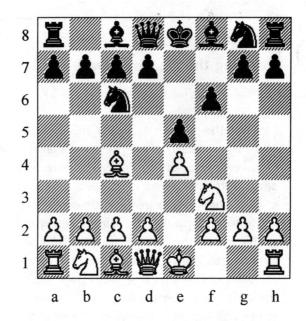

WHITE TO MOVE

One way to reach this position is by **1. e4 e5   2. Nf3 Nc6   3. Bc4 f6?.** Not only is Black's last move unnecessary, it's terribly weakening, since White's king-bishop sits on a diagonal that cuts right through the center into Black's heart at f7 and g8.

The move f7-f6 also impedes Black's queen and dark-square bishop, while depriving the king-knight of its optimal square. After **4. d4,** Black will have difficulty completing his development and satisfying the security needs of his king.

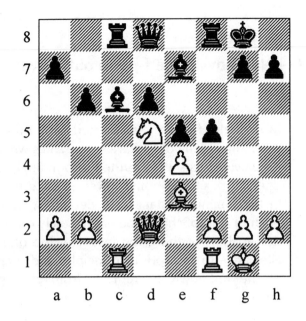

WHITE TO MOVE

This position illustrates another questionable f-pawn move. In trying to undermine White's knight, and to obtain play along the f-file for his king-rook, Black has just played the sharp 1. . . . **f7-f5?**, which on the surface is more reasonable than the f-pawn advance in the previous example.

This sometimes risky f-pawn pincer looks particularly malevolent in that it threatens 2. . . . f4, trapping White's queen-bishop. But f7-f5 also opens the a2-g8 diagonal, leading to Black's own king. Before Black gets the chance to play f5-f4, two incisive captures burst his bubble: **2. Nxe7+ Qxe7 3. Rxc6! Rxc6 4. Qd5+**, and White regains the rook, putting him a solid piece up.

30

AILMENT:

Not moving the f-pawn out of fear.

Moving the f-pawn is associated with a number of problems. Many of us have seen games where early KB-pawn thrusts were refuted resoundingly. But this doesn't mean we should never advance the f-pawn in the beginning stages. All decisions, whether to push or not to, should be based solely on an objective analysis of the given instance. Too often blind allegiance to amorphous principles and simple fear of the unknown prevent us from playing good moves.

Rx

1. Think over your initial impulses.
2. Don't yield to them at once, but don't ignore them.
3. If you want to move the f-pawn sharply, dispassionately balance its merits and demerits.
4. If its pluses seem to outweigh its minuses (we can never be sure), forge on.
5. Be objective. Don't submit to fear or prejudice. If an idea seems right, do it.
6. Don't let failure in previous games influence you.
7. If you fail to seize the moment, your opponent will seize it.

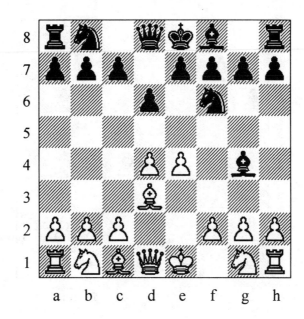

WHITE TO MOVE

Our fear of moving the f-pawn, even in entirely justifiable circumstances, often gets us into unpleasant situations. For example, after **1. e4 d6   2. d4 Nf6   3. Bd3 Bg4?** (diagram), White must respond to the threat against his queen.

The best move is 4. f3, which compels the bishop to retreat. White thereby gains time while strengthening his e-pawn. But because of the standard injunctions against early f-pawn moves, White could be intimidated into replying 4. Nf3?, putting the king-knight in an irksome pin. One mistake negates the other.

30b

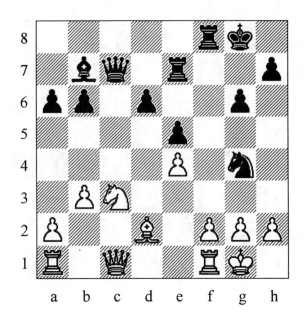

WHITE TO MOVE

Not surprisingly, f-pawn fear can blind us to very desirable, but disguised, tactics. In this position, White would like to drive out Black's knight with f2-f3, buttressing his e-pawn. He sees, however, that Black's queen would then have a ghastly check at c5, leading to material gain.

But if White looks a little further ahead, he might find that that after **1. f3 Qc5+? 2. Kh1 Nf2+ 3. Rxf2 Qxf2 4. Be3!**, Black must lose material, for **4. ... Qh4** is countered by the forking **5. Bg5!**.

31

Blocking the c-pawn in certain openings.

In order to get play against the opponent's center in d-pawn games and flank openings, it's often necessary to advance the c-pawn, releasing your queen and attacking the opponent's Q4 square. Without this thrust, it's practically impossible to soften up the opponent's central formation. The problems set in when you develop the queen-knight to QB3 before moving the c-pawn, preventing the pawn from moving at all.

Rx

1. In most queen-pawn games and flank openings, avoid prematurely blocking the c-pawn.
2. Determine if it could be a weapon against the enemy center.
3. Consider advancing it without direct protection.
4. Don't be afraid to rely on indirect defenses.
5. In your home analyses, acquaint yourself with the typical ways to win back captured c-pawns.
6. For example, remember the moves Q-QR4, N-QR3, N-K5, and P-QR4 to undermine the enemy's protective b-pawn.
7. If your c-pawn is taken, aim to gain control of the center, especially your K4.
8. Play practice games where you offer the c-pawn soundly. Then try to get it back.

31

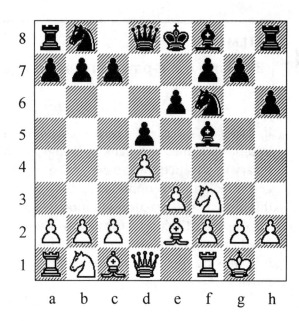

In this position, which develops from **1. d4 d5   2. Nf3 Nf6   3. e3 Bf5   4. Be2 e6   5. 0-0 h6,** Black is playing to control e4 by guarding that square three times. If White is to get play, he should advance the c-pawn two squares.

The developing move **6. Nc3?** is a mistake. Though it attacks the center, it doesn't mount a real threat to d5, nor does it meaningfully prepare the e-pawn for further movement to e4.

This knight jump actually thwarts White's own chances by blocking the c-pawn. Now White can't open lines for his queen and queen-rook, and he can expect difficulty trying to obtain central activity.

32

Automatically playing B-N5 to attack a knight.

A typical terrorist attack has a bishop going to knight-five, hitting an enemy knight on bishop-three. This might pin the knight, preventing or discouraging its movement. Sometimes, however, the attacked knight can boomerang and move anyhow, and the once-aggressive bishop suddenly finds itself on the defensive. And there are instances where the bishop could be assailed by a pawn, forcing it to move again. Bishop-to-knight-five is often a good move, but don't always count on it.

Rx

1. Don't play B-N5 attacking a knight without knowing how you will respond if your opponent's rook-pawn "puts the question to your bishop."
2. Decide ahead of time whether you will retreat or take the knight.
3. If he does play P-R3, analyze the situation again, just to be sure.
4. Before playing B-N5, also determine if your opponent can then move the knight to threaten the bishop.
5. Think twice about B-N5 if it doesn't actually pin the knight.
6. Even when B-N5 pins the knight, watch out for a pin-breaking sacrifice.
7. If your opponent hits you with B-N5, frustrate or deflect him from his plans.

32a

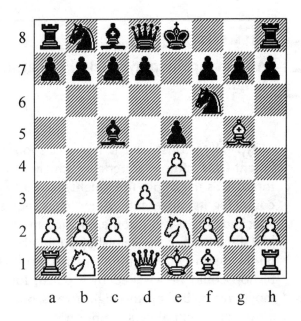

BLACK TO MOVE

Here's an example of an ill-considered B-N5 move. The position arises after **1. e4 e5   2. Ne2 Nf6   3. d3 Bc5   4. Bg5?.**

Here, Bg5 is a pedestrian pin that actually doesn't work, for **4. . . . Nxe4!** gains at least a pawn. If 5. Bxd8, then 5. . . . Bxf2 is mate. Thus White must submit to 5. dxe4 Qxg5.

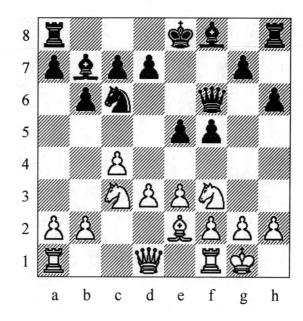

32b

BLACK TO MOVE

Another punchless bishop attack is seen in this diagram, where Black plays **1. . . . Bb4.** The c3-knight then turns it around on the assailing bishop with **2. Nd5,** forking queen, b4-bishop, and c7-pawn. After **2. . . . Qd8** (2. . . . Qd6 is met by 3. a3), White gains a pawn by either 3. Nxb4 Nxb4 4. Nxe5 or even 3. Nxe5 at once.

32c

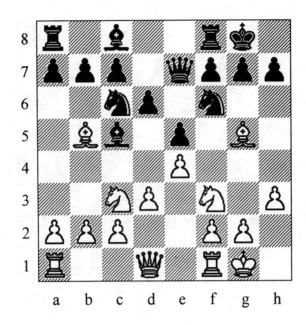

BLACK TO MOVE

Finally, in Problem 32c, Black should play **1. . . . Be6,** guarding against **2. Nd5.** Instead he creates a symmetrical array of minor pieces with **1. . . . Bb4?,** a redeployment that ignores the demolishing **2. Nd5.** However Black responds, he must lose material.

For example, if **2. . . . Qd8,** then **3. Bxf6 gxf6 4. Bxc6 bxc6 5. Nxb4** looks good. The message should be clear. The routine move bishop-to-knight-five is not always a good idea, even when it pins a knight.

33

Creating a self-pin with an enemy bishop on knight-five.

When your opponent's bishop moves to its knight-five, attacking your unpinned bishop-three knight, you fall into the enemy's game plan if you move the center pawn, putting your own knight in a pin. This is often an automatic response, in some cases played to defend the knight with the queen, but it allows your opponent to establish the pin he didn't deserve to get.

Rx

1. If an enemy bishop attacks your knight, see if you can move your knight to attack the bishop.
2. Avoid self-pinning your knights.
3. For example, if Black's c8-bishop moves to g4, attacking White's f3-knight, White shouldn't move the e2-pawn without considering the possibility of playing Nf3-e5, attacking the bishop.
4. If that counter seems to work, he should play it instead of moving the e-pawn.
5. Don't answer bad moves with bad responses.

33

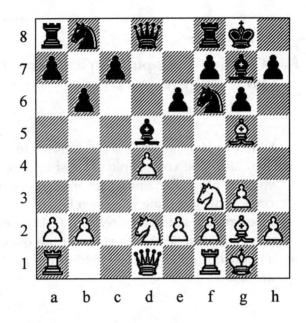

WHITE TO MOVE

Black has just advanced his e-pawn one square, which ineptly self-pins his f6-knight. It costs Black a piece after **1. e4!**. If Black retreats the d5-bishop to safety, the f6-knight is nailed by e4-e5.

34

Placing a bishop where it can be driven back by pawns.

It's natural in an aggressive game like chess to move a bishop across the frontier line into enemy territory. But if such a move is not connected to a particular purpose, it could wind up costing time, especially when the intrusive bishop can be driven back by pawns. True, these pawn attacks sometimes incur enemy weaknesses and produce potential targets, so the bishop's invasion is not in vain. But often enough a bishop so moved is misdirected and simply wastes time. It will have to move again, without any great inconvenience on the opponent's part, and you could lose the initiative.

Rx

1. Don't move bishops across the frontier line without definite purpose and without first considering the consequences.
2. If you're doing it to inflict pawn weaknesses on your opponent, make sure it's really worthwhile.
3. Don't emphasize small points to the neglect of more serious concerns, such as king safety and development.
4. Avoid giving your opponent ready targets.
5. Expel advanced enemy pieces with dispatch.

34a

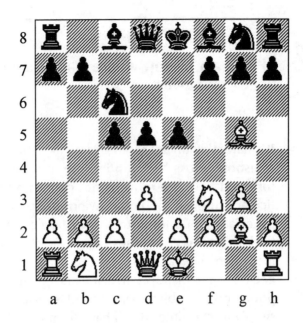

BLACK TO MOVE

The next few positions show unjustified bishop attacks being countered by pawn blocks. In Problem 34a, arrived at after **1. Nf3 d5 2. g3 c5 3. Bg2 Nc6 4. d3 e5 5. Bg5?**, White attacks Black's queen, but not desirably, for **5. . . . f6** blocks the threat with an initiative-stealing move.

34b

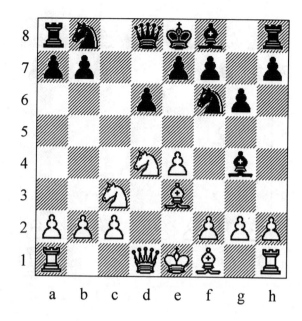

WHITE TO MOVE

This position from a Dragon Sicilian (**1. e4 c5   2. Nf3 d6   3. d4 cxd4   4. Nxd4 Nf6   5. Nc3 g6   6. Be3 Bg4?**), is a similar situation. Black attacks White's queen, but White rebuffs the attack with a gain of time by **7. f3**. As in the previous example, the blocking pawn also strengthens the center.

34c

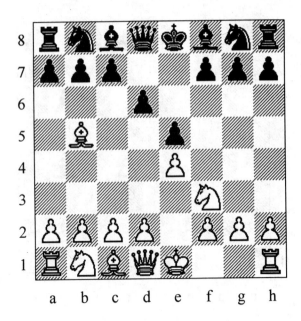

BLACK TO MOVE

In this situation, after the moves **1. e4 e5   2. Nf3 d6   3. Bb5 +,** White develops the bishop with check. But rather than gaining time, the move actually loses time to **3. . . . c6.** This nullifies the threat and forces the bishop to move again, gaining a tempo. Answer a bad attack with a good defense and the initiative is yours.

35

AILMENT:

Failing to complete a fianchetto.

Once you've moved a knight-pawn in order to flank the bishop on that wing, the squares to the side of the knight-pawn are weakened. Moreover, advancing the knight-pawn often exposes a rook in the corner to potential threats. By not completing the fianchetto, you leave the cornered rook and the weakened squares susceptible to tactics, especially if your opponent can occupy the diagonal first.

Rx

1. Don't fianchetto without understanding the position.
2. If you start to flank your bishop, finish it.
3. Don't waste time, allowing your opponent to beat you to the punch on the flanking diagonal.
4. Don't play frivolous in-between moves.
5. If your opponent instigates a fianchetto against you, try to divert him from finishing the job.
6. Try to trade off the enemy fianchettoed bishop.

35a

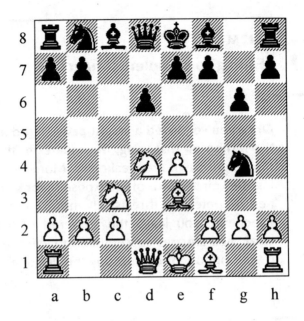

WHITE TO MOVE

This position is reached after the moves **1. e4 c5 2. Nf3 d6 3. d4 cxd4 4. Nxd4 Nf6 5. Nc3 g6 6. Be3 Ng4?.**

White now wins material with **7. Bb5 + !,** when 7. . . . . Nc6 loses to 8. Nxc6 bxc6 9. Bxc6 + , while 7. . . . . Bd7 is answered by the merciless 8. Qxg4!. Black could have avoided this loss by completing his fianchetto with 6. . . . . Bg7.

35b

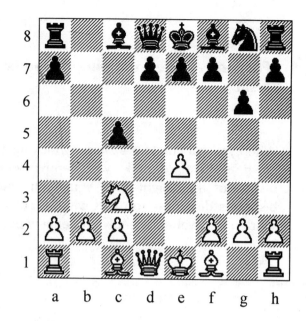

WHITE TO MOVE

A humorous illustration of this mistake is Problem 35b. On the previous move, instead of following through on his intended fianchetto, 1. . . . Bg7, Black blundered with **1. . . . c5?.** White now wins with **2. Qd5! Rb8   3. Qe5!,** forking the clowning rooks.

AILMENT:

Flanking and self-trapping the other bishop.

When you fianchetto a bishop by moving a knight-pawn to its third rank, you deprive your other bishop of the knight-three square. If your other bishop is developed on that wing, it could be ensnarled in a web of friendly and enemy pawns.

Rx

1. Whenever you have a bishop developed on a particular wing—either at knight-five, bishop-four, or rook-four—be extra concerned before fianchettoing the other bishop.
2. Determine if there's a safe retreat.
3. See if you'll have the time to trade the bishop for an enemy minor piece before your opponent's pawns trap it.
4. Generally, avoid placing your pieces where they get in the way of your other pieces.
5. Have a temporary plan of where all the pieces might go before moving any of them.
6. Modify your plans as the game develops.

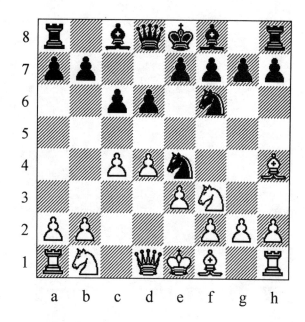

WHITE TO MOVE

In this somewhat unusual position, arrived at after **1. d4 Nf6   2. Bg5 Ne4   3. Bh4 d6   4. Nf3 Nbd7   5. c4 c6   6. e3 Ndf6,** White should develop the queen-knight (say to d2) or the king-bishop (say to d3 or e2).

But fianchettoing the king-bishop, **7. g3?,** is simply wrong. Why waste time and create weaknesses developing a piece that could be brought out at once without incurring any problems? Now the h4-bishop is without safe retreat, since the g3-pawn blocks the way.

Black wins a piece by **7. . . . g5!,** when **8. Nxg5 Nxg5   9. Bxg5** fails to **9. . . . Qa5 +,** forking king and bishop.

PART TWO

CAPTURES, RECAPTURES, AND EXCHANGES

37

AILMENT:

Trading when behind in material.

You've just lost a piece, and you mindlessly exchange off your remaining forces. This is the surest way to lose. If you have a material disadvantage, trading down tends to accentuate the disparity. Being ahead 10 to 9 is not as great a superiority as 2 to 1. With each trade the ratio improves for the attacker. Eventually, his extra material will win.

Rx

1. When behind, avoid trades unless there's a compelling reason.
2. Don't play variations that are likely to result in trades later on.
3. Keep the position complicated to pull a swindle.
4. Strive to confuse your opponent.
5. Create counterplay.
6. Especially go after the enemy king.

37

White thinks he can trade, reasoning that **1. Rd3** leads to a draw. If 1. . . . Rxd3+, then 2. Kxd3 gives White the opposition, and Black can't force the promotion of his pawn.

A sample variation is 2. . . . Kc5   3. Kc3 d5   4. Kd3 d4   5. Kd2 Kc4   6. Kc2 d3+   7. Kd2 Kd4   8. Kd1 Ke3   9. Ke1 d2+   10. Kd1 Kd3 stalemate.

Unfortunately, in response to 1. Rd3, Black can shift tempo with the zwischenzug **1. . . . Ke4!** (or 1. . . . Kc4!). White must then exchange rooks, **2. Rxd4+ Kxd4**, and Black gets a meaningful opposition that can be used to force a win.

The final moves might be 3. Ke2 Kc3 (a turning maneuver) 4. Kd1 d4   5. Kc1 d3   6. Kd1 d2 (advancing the pawn to the 7th without giving check!) 7. Ke2 Kc2 and wins.

38

AILMENT:

Avoiding advantageous trades when ahead in material.

This is the corollary to the previous situation. By ignoring exchanges when ahead, you allow your opponent to stay in the game. The longer he is permitted to hang around, the more opportunities he has to save himself. If he has less material because you've been trading, he has fewer chances to complicate and escape.

Of course, there are times when you shouldn't trade even though you're ahead, such as when you're pressing a mating attack and you think you've got him.

Rx

1. When ahead, trade pieces ruthlessly.
2. Simplify the position until the correct strategy is clear.
3. Defuse enemy counterattacking possibilities.
4. Emphasize your advantages.
5. Don't waste time on irrelevancies.
6. For practice, play out resigned positions to mate.
7. Remember that boring positions can often be valuable to study. They don't become boring until you know them.

38

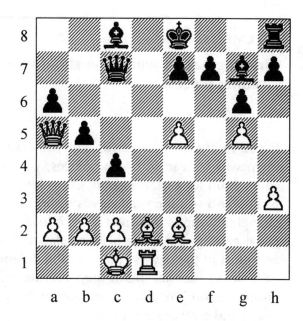

In this position, Black is ahead by a pawn, though his king is still in the center and perhaps subject to threats. White is offering a trade of queens, which Black should accept and then castle. After Black castles, two of White's pawns would be under fire (at e5 and h3).

But instead of swapping down, Black greedily consumes a pawn, **1. . . . Qxe5?,** also threatening mate at b2. But this violation of strategy costs him the game: **2. Qd8 + ! Kxd8   3. Ba5 + Ke8   4. Rd8#.**

39

AILMENT:

Trading pawns when you should be trading pieces.

If you're ahead by a pawn, and you trade pawns for pawns instead of trading pieces, you're setting yourself up for a drawn game. Consider the case of bishop and seven pawns versus bishop and six. Exchanging bishops is correct if it produces a winning pawn ending. But if the bishops stay on the board and most of the pawns come off, the defender may be able to sacrifice his bishop for the remaining pawns, leaving insufficient mating material on the board and a theoretical draw.

Rx

1. When ahead, trade pieces.
2. Even when trying to swap pieces, don't give up active ones for inactive ones, unless it makes your job easier.
3. Don't trade pieces you need.
4. When trying to realize an advantage, aim to have pieces of different types. If your opponent has a knight, keep a bishop.
5. Try to retain pawns on both flanks of the board to reduce the possibility of drawing sacrifices.

39

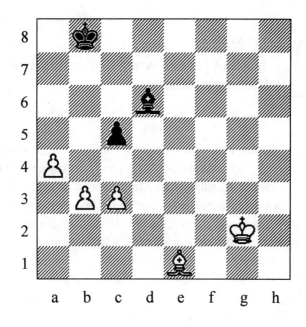

White is ahead by two pawns. The correct strategy is to trade the remaining pieces by 1. Bg3, reducing to an easily won pawn ending. Instead, loosely following the principle of trading when ahead, White plays **1. b4?,** wrongly offering to trade pawns.

After **1. . . . cxb4 2. cxb4,** Black can use the opportunity to swap down to a positional draw by surrendering his bishop for White's b-pawn, **2. . . . Bxb4! 3. Bxb4.** Up a bishop and pawn at that point, White has no way to force the Black king out of the corner. White's dark-square bishop simply can't control a8.

40

Trading pieces when you should be trading pawns.

If you're behind in material and you start trading pieces, you're helping your opponent. You need pieces to guard your pawns and to create complications. If you must trade pieces, consider if it leads to a book draw or a position where a draw is more likely, as in endgames with bishops of opposite colors.

Rx

1. When behind in material, trade pawns, not pieces.
2. Especially exchange off weak or beleaguered pawns so that you no longer have to tie down your pieces defending them.
3. Trade pawns if it results in a position where you can sacrifice your last minor piece for your opponent's last pawn to establish a draw by insufficient mating material.
4. For practice, set up endgames where you are a pawn ahead or behind, and play them out against a friend. You play the winning side in one game, your friend in the next.
5. Set a five-minute-per-side time limit and play at least ten games with the same position or slightly modified ones.
6. Remember that in some cases it may be more important to stop the opponent's plans than to fulfill your own.

40

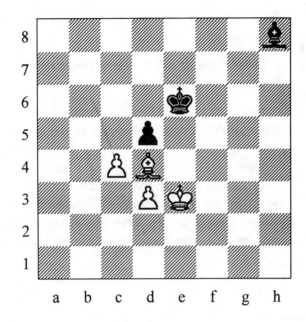

Black is behind by a pawn, and his bishop is threatened. So he trades it to save it, **1. . . . Bxd4 + ? 2. Kxd4.** Funny thing is, this loses after **2. . . . dxc4 3. Kxc4! Kd6 4. Kd4** (taking the opposition) **Kc6** (4. . . . Ke6 5. Kc5) **5. Ke5.**

With this turning maneuver, White's king heads for e6, a critical square, and the pawn soon promotes: **5. . . . Kd7 6. Kd5 Ke7 7. Kc6 Kd8 8. d4 Kc8 9. d5 Kd8 10. Kd6 Ke8** (or 10. . . . Kc8 11. Ke7) **11. Kc7** and wins.

Black could have drawn by trading pawns instead, **1. . . . dxc4!,** when 2. Bxh8 cxd3 3. Kxd3 leaves White with insufficient mating material. So White must respond 2. dxc4, after which Black then trades bishops, **2. . . . Bxd4 + 3. Kxd4,** and draws by taking the opposition, **3. . . . Kd6.**

41

AILMENT:

Taking back with the wrong unit.

This applies especially to situations in which there are two ways to recapture, and neither seems better on the surface. You mistakenly focus on the act of recapturing rather than which way it's done. But even in the most "obvious" situations, little differences could mean everything. It doesn't appear to matter until you take the wrong way, and suddenly it does.

Rx

1. Recapture as flexibly as possible, retaining the most options.
2. If there are several ways to recapture, analyze each one.
3. If there are no obvious choices, examine small points.
4. Consider pawn structure, open lines, defense, and overall coordination.
5. For practice, make lists of these positional small points and arrange them by category.
6. From time to time, review them and refine your classifications.
7. Use your opponent's time to evaluate captures and exchanges.
8. But when it's actually your move and you must take back, double-check your analysis.
9. Try to outmaneuver your opponent into undesirable exchanges.

41

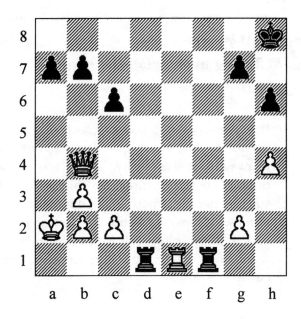

BLACK TO MOVE

Things could be very bad for White here, especially if Black captures White's rook with the correct rook. If 1. . . . . Rdxe1!, White cannot avert mate at a1 without sacrificing his queen.

Note that the position of White's queen closes out two potential escape squares: b4, blocked by the queen, and b3, occupied by an unmovable pawn.

But if Black indiscriminately takes on e1 with the other rook, **1. . . . . Rfxe1?,** White's queen can safely check on f8, gaining a tempo so that White can follow with b3-b4, clearing an escape hatch for his king. Thus the wrong capture lets the opponent off the hook.

42

In some situations you can take with either of two pawns: One capture is toward the center, the other is away from the center. Taking toward the center often increases central control, so that important squares are guarded and supported. Taking the other way, however, tends to increase pawn islands, making it more difficult for pawns to be defended. It might also help your opponent obtain a useful pawn majority.

Rx

1. In most situations, take toward the center.
2. But be sure to consider the opposite possibility.
3. Especially determine if taking away from the center gives you an unexpected resource.
4. For practice, whenever you come upon a diagram from a master game, try to imagine the board with only pawns, without pieces.
5. If you can't quite do this, set up the corresponding pawn skeleton on your own board.
6. In your own games, when planning, use pawn formations as guidelines.

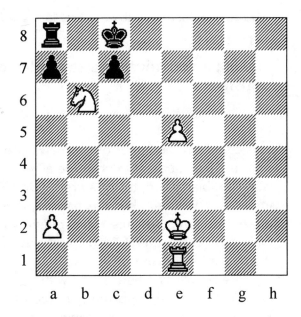

BLACK TO MOVE

White has just captured on b6, giving check, and Black has two ways to recapture. He can take back toward the center, **1. . . . axb6!,** or he can take away from the center, 1. . . . cxb6?.

Capturing away from the center enables White to retain his material, while 1. . . . axb6, opening the a-file for the rook, gains a pawn, for 2. Ra1 Ra5 immediately purges the e-pawn (3. e6 is met by 3. . . . Re5 +).

43

AILMENT:

Taking automatically to straighten one's pawns.

This applies when either of two pawns can capture on the same square. One capture eliminates an existing doubled pawn, the other retains it. The natural impulse is to undouble the pawn and repair the pawn structure. But this often requires capturing away from the center, which could actually reduce the dynamism in your position.

An example is when Black, with pawns on a7, c7 and c6, has the opportunity to recapture on b6. Playing c7xb6 straightens his pawns but loses control of d6 and doesn't open any lines. Playing a7xb6 opens the a-file and makes his pawns more compact, still keeping his hold on d6.

Rx

1. Don't routinely recapture to straighten your pawns, especially if it means taking away from the center.
2. In general, however, doubled pawns should be avoided.
3. But consider whether keeping doubled pawns leads to increased attacking possibilities.
4. Determine whether your pawns will then be easier or harder to defend.
5. Decide which way of recapturing gives greater flexibility.
6. Don't emphasize eliminating doubled pawns and disregard everything else.

43

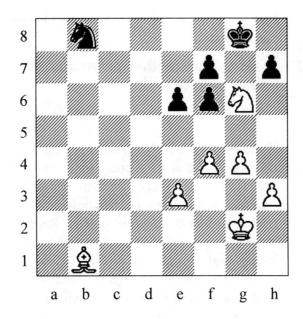

BLACK TO MOVE

Black has two ways to take back here. The right way is toward the center, 1. . . . hxg6, and even though it doesn't undouble Black's pawns, it gives him a compact, easy-to-defend structure.

Straightening the pawn structure by taking away from the center actually loses material, for **1. . . . fxg6?   2. Ba2 Kf7   3. f5 gxf5   4. gxf5** wins the e-pawn because of the pin.

44

AILMENT:

Taking back with a pawn and obstructing a key square or line.

If you recapture with a pawn, the square you capture on is blocked and, at least temporarily, unusable. That is, you can't occupy it with pieces. Nor can you then easily move the obstructing pawn to make the square available to your pieces. Pawns are easily blocked, and even when they can move, their advance might entail risk and real concessions, such as the weakening of nearby squares. This is one problem capturing with a pawn induces. Pieces, on the other hand, can often be shifted without incurring weakness or changing a position's basic character.

Rx

1. If you want continued access to a square, try to recapture on it with a piece.
2. Do this by overprotecting the square with several pieces and pawns.
3. Defend so that you have options. Don't get locked into a situation.
4. As a rule, if you have a number of pieces defending a point and the number is just sufficient, add an extra protector to free any of the defending pieces for other activity.

44

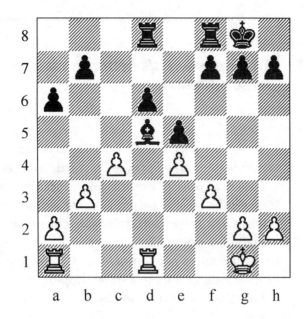

WHITE TO MOVE

There are three ways for White to take back on d5: with the c-pawn, the e-pawn, or the d1-rook. But only one way allows White continued use of the d-file, and that's **1. Rxd5.** Thereafter White will double rooks on the d-file and prepare to advance the c-pawn at the right moment.

45

Trading when it's better to maintain a tense situation.

In many instances, it's a mistake to declare your intentions with an exchange. Instead, by keeping the situation alive, you prevent your opponent from going ahead with his own plans. He will be unable to release his units from defensive chores, upholding threatened points. If you exchange, his forces are freed for more active pursuits. It's not unusual for neither side to initiate a trade, hoping the adversary will declare his intentions by being the first to take.

Rx

1. Don't trade if it reduces your scope or options.
2. Avoid instigating a particular exchange that liberates or unfetters your opponent's pieces.
3. Don't trade if it loses the initiative.
4. Avoid trades when you're better developed.
5. Pressure your opponent into making bad exchanges.
6. When watching or playing over games between strong players, take note of all the unforced exchanges, and determine who comes out on top: the player taking or the one taking back.

45

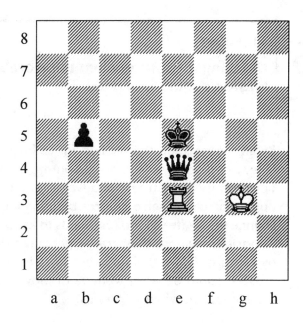

This position shows the value of sitting on an exchange until the time is right. If White captures Black's queen at once, 1. Rxe4+ Kxe4, he won't be able to catch the pawn, for 2. Kf2 Kd3 3. Ke1 Kc2 shuts him out.

Since the queen is pinned and can't run away, White uses the tempo to bring his king closer, **1. Kf2!**. If 1. . . . Qxe3+, then 2. Kxe3 gives White the opposition with a draw. Meanwhile, 1. . . . Kd4 is answered by 2. Rxe4+ Kxe4 3. Ke2, also drawing by means of the opposition.

There follows **1. . . . b4 2. Ke2!**, milking the pin for another move, because 2. . . . Qxe3+ 3. Kxe3 is still a draw.

The last try is **2. . . . b3,** but that gets nowhere after **3. Kd1!,** when 3. . . . Qxe3 is a stalemate, and 3. . . . b2 4. Rxe4+ Kxe4 5. Kc2 catches the pawn. By not taking the queen and maintaining the tension of the pin, White was able to gain enough time to save himself.

46

AILMENT:
Delaying a capture when unfavorable tension should be ended.

By all means keep the tension for as long as desirable, but if you wait too long, you might miss your opportunity to capture with advantage. Worse, your opponent could seize control by initiating the exchange first. After all, no one wants to keep his units in positions where they are perpetually threatened by capture. If the drain on resources becomes too great, it could be wiser to trade or move away. The art is knowing when to do this.

Rx

1. Review all reasonable exchanges on each move.
2. Don't assume that because retaining the tension is good on one move, it must be good on the next.
3. Don't play moves based on previous assumptions.
4. If your opponent seems to be sitting on a possible exchange, set him up, and then beat him to the punch.
5. If you know the position well, don't rush your moves if there's a chance your opponent might fall into a trap. Let him think you're confused so that he lets down his guard.

46

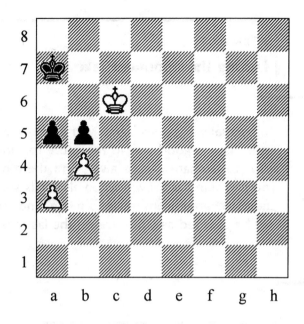

BLACK TO MOVE

The opposite of releasing tension too soon is maintaining it too long, which is the situation of Problem 46. In order to draw, Black merely has to exchange pawns, 1. . . . axb4   2. axb4, and play his king back to a8 or b8. Whenever White takes the b5-pawn with his king, Black seizes the opposition with Kb7 and holds.

But if Black tries to hold everything with the tension-preserving **1. . . . Ka6?**, then White insures a winning passed pawn by **2. a4!**, for 2. . . . bxa4 loses to 3. b5 + Ka7   4. Kc7 a3   5. b6 + Ka6   6. b7 a2   7. b8/Q a1/Q   8. Qb6# (or 8. Qb7#).

Nor is 2. . . . axb4 any better because of 3. axb5 + Ka5   4. b6 b3   5. b7, and White queens first.

47

AILMENT:
Letting the opponent take first.

This usually happens when you are sufficiently secure, have a good way to recapture for now, don't want to exchange right away, and therefore think you can stand pat. Even when all this is so, circumstances change from move to move, and you might not be covered as you were on the last move.

Rx

1. Don't let your opponent take first if it allows him to control the exchanging situation.
2. Trade pieces when the initiative is at stake and the concomitant tactics seem to lend support.
3. Maintain your position if you can recapture with advantage.
4. Take to avoid material loss.
5. If you truly can't decide whether to trade, maintain the tension, or move the attacked piece to safety, just take the opponent's piece.
6. Always check plans made earlier before you implement them later.

47

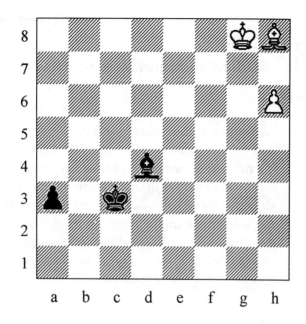

BLACK TO MOVE

Black sees that his bishop is guarded, so he feels no urgency to initiate a trade and pushes ahead with his plan: to make a new queen. But after **1. . . . a2?** (letting White control the capture by taking first) **2. Bxd4+ Kxd4   3. h7 a1/Q   4. h8/Q+,** Black loses his queen even though he has queened first.

The correct idea is to take first, **1. . . . Bxh8!**, and after **2. Kxh8 a2   3. h7 a1/Q   4. Kg8,** the game should end in a draw. Black's king is not close enough to join the queen in time to weave a mating net.

48

Trading and thereby surrendering a file.

Rooks need open files to attack the enemy position and to threaten to move into the enemy camp. So it's not uncommon for a player to shift a rook to an open file, backed up by his other rook. In order to stop the incursion—let's say to the seventh rank—the opponent might transfer a rook of his own to the same file, supported by his other rook. Thus, if either player takes the opponent's rook, the player taking back gets control of the file.

Rx

1. Don't exchange rooks if it abandons a file, unless you have no choice.
2. Avoid putting yourself into such a situation by looking ahead.
3. Instead of trading rooks, see if your rook can occupy an anchor point on the same file.
4. In this way, try to force an exchange that improves your position.
5. If your opponent doesn't take, move another rook to the file on the next move, doubling rooks.
6. Once you have control of a file, use it to invade the enemy position.

48a

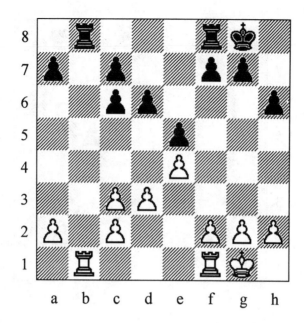

WHITE TO MOVE

This position is virtually symmetrical. There is only one open file, the b-file, and both sides occupy it with a rook, preventing the opponent from using the file.

White could try to exploit the b-file by **1. Rb3**, which prepares doubling rooks with **2. Rfb1**. If Black counters with **1. . . . Rxb3**, White replies **2. axb3**, opening the a-file for attack against a7.

It would be a mistake, however, to abandon the file with **1. Rxb8?**, when **1. . . . Rxb8** threatens penetration at b2, leading to the gain of at least a pawn.

48b

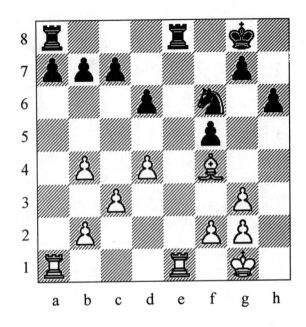

WHITE TO MOVE

In Problem 48b, the e-file is neutralized by opposing rooks, while White has control of the a-file. He should simply ready his forces for the ensuing ending, possibly with 1. Kf1.

But trying to win the a-pawn by ceding the e-file would be a mistake, for **1. Rxe8 Rxe8 2. Rxa7?** loses by force to **2. ... Re1+ 3. Kh2 Ng4+ 4. Kh3 Rh1#.**

49

Automatically opposing rooks.

When the opponent seizes an open file with a rook, inertia leads us to grab a share of the file by moving a rook of our own onto it. This usually works when our own rooks are connected, so that if one is captured, the other can replace it. But this might fail if it draws the second rook, the protective one, out of position to fulfill another function. If the rooks aren't connected, we wind up losing control of the file anyway.

Rx

1. Certainly oppose rooks when you're sure the consequences are favorable.
2. If they're not, instead of opposing rooks, look to open a file of your own.
3. Neutralize your opponent's use of the first file by using a different file.
4. Make sure your rooks remain active.
5. Look several moves ahead before making commitments.
6. If you can't refute your opponent's plans, dodge them.
7. Avoid purely defensive play.

49

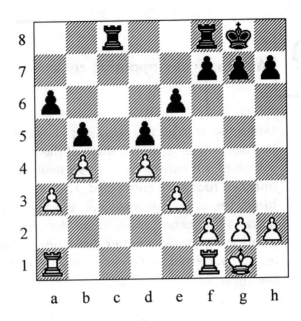

WHITE TO MOVE

White's natural impulse here is to oppose rooks on the c-file with **1. Rfc1?**. But this is met by the anchoring **1. . . . Rc4**, preparing to double rooks. And if **2. Rxc4**, Black gets a supported passed pawn by **2. . . . bxc4** (or even 2. . . . dxc4).

Rather than opposing rooks, White should try to get his own open file with **1. a4!**, when **1. . . . Rc4** is answered by **2. Rfb1**.

50

Developing a piece costs a tempo. If you then exchange your developed piece (let's say a bishop) for an unmoved enemy piece (like a knight) still sitting on its back row, and your opponent recaptures, thereby developing a rook, you've lost time. It costs you two tempi to trade off the bishop and you have nothing to show for it. Meanwhile, your opponent has developed a rook without having had to waste time developing the captured knight. It's a poor deal for you.

Rx

1. Don't bring your pieces out with the idea of immediately trading them off.
2. The only time you should ever seek such trades is if the course of play unexpectedly warrants it; for example, if your opponent blunders.
3. Instead, try to find effective squares for your pieces, with an eye toward long-term influence and activity.
4. Put your pieces where they do the most good.
5. Make sure your pieces and pawns are in harmony.

50

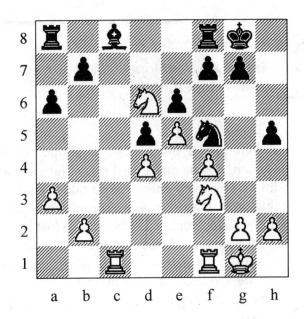

WHITE TO MOVE

This position looks pretty good for White. He has a stalwart knight at d6 and absolute control of the c-file. An excellent way to increase his advantage is 1. Rc7, seizing the seventh rank, when 1. . . . Nxd6 2. exd6 Rd8 3. Rfc1 is very strong.

But **1. Nxc8?**, trading his lofty knight for an undeveloped and scopeless bishop, is an error, for after **1. . . . Raxc8** Black will have no trouble holding.

Black could even do a lot better, for the mechanical **2. Rc5?**, preparing to double rooks, drops a pawn to **2. . . . Nxd4! 3. Rxc8 Nxf3+ 4. Rxf3 Rxc8.**

51

Aimlessly trading and dissipating your attack.

If you are on the attack, exchanging pieces can weaken your plans, whether material or positional, since you thereby have fewer units with which to combine. Here you are, about to play the winning move, and you suddenly realize you've already traded the piece you need.

Rx

1. Don't trade when pressing an attack.
2. If you must avoid trades by moving away, do so with a gain of time.
3. Steer clear of trades when better developed.
4. If trying to avoid trades, look out for cross checks, pins, and other simplifying strategems.
5. Analyze several moves ahead to avert potential problems.
6. Pretend you are your opponent trying to refute your own moves.

51

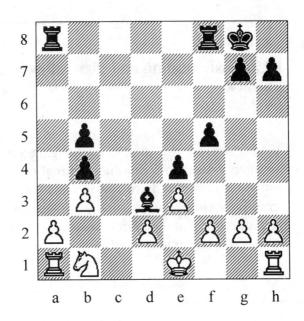

BLACK TO MOVE

Black's game is obviously superior to White's. None of White's pieces are developed, and the d3-bishop prevents White from castling. One winning idea for Black is to double rooks on the c-file and threaten mate at c1. There is no satisfactory defense to this.

But Black trades good bishop for bad knight just to win a pawn, **1. . . . Bxb1?,** and after **2. Rxb1 Rxa2   3. Ke2 Rfd8   4. Rhd1,** White has excellent chances to survive.

52

If you opt not to trade, and you move a piece out of attack arbitrarily, you lose time. You sacrifice at least a move, which could be used to press the initiative, build your game, or enable a defense to be set up, and you might be sacrificing even more than that.

Rx

1. Trade when you can't afford to waste time.
2. Trade when you need to gain time.
3. Trade to maintain the initiative.
4. Don't allow the situation to stand if it lets your opponent control the exchange.
5. If you must move, try to do so with a threat, so that your opponent can't build his game at your expense.
6. Don't retain pieces for subjective reasons if the position requires exchanges.

52a

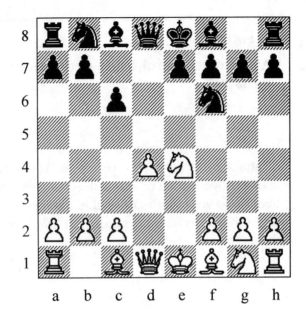

WHITE TO MOVE

This position comes from the Caro-Kann Defense after the moves **1. e4 c6 2. d4 d5 3. Nc3 dxe4 4. Nxe4 Nf6.** White's knight is threatened, and the best way to cope with the threat is to exchange knights, when White maintains the initiative.

52b

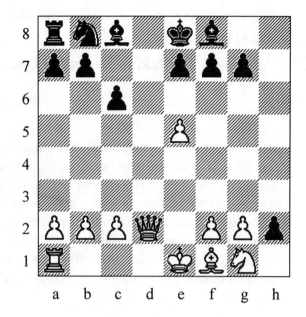

WHITE RESIGNS

But the retreat **5. Ng3,** though playable, enables Black to become aggressive. A famous trap is **5. . . . h5   6. Bg5 h4   7. Bxf6? hxg3   8. Be5 Rxh2   9. Rxh2 Qa5 +   10. Qd2 Qxe5 +!   11. dxe5 gxh2** (see diagram), and Black gets the queen back with interest.

53

AILMENT:

Automatically taking to double opposing pawns.

In a perfect chess world, doubled pawns are bad. The front one blocks the back one, snarling traffic along the file. Furthermore, neither doubled pawn can defend the other, as when they're on adjacent files. But in real chess, doubled pawns cannot be judged bad without considering attendant circumstances. In fact, in many instances, the inflicting of doubled pawns makes concessions that aren't worth the ploy.

Rx

1. Don't go out of your way to give your opponent doubled pawns.
2. First make a mental balance sheet of pluses and minuses.
3. If the negative seems to eclipse the positive, change your plans.
4. Don't emphasize the trivial over the really important. Create doubled pawns, but not if it lets you get mated.
5. Don't base an analysis on superficial considerations.

53a

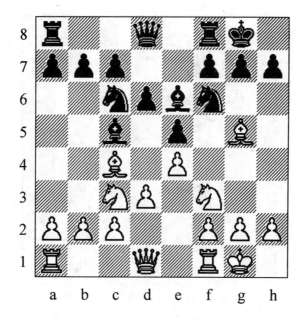

WHITE TO MOVE

This is a standard position reached after the moves **1. e4 e5 2. Nf3 Nc6 3. Bc4 Bc5 4. Nc3 Nf6 5. d3 d6 6. 0-0 0-0 7. Bg5 Be6.**

White has a pin on the f6-knight, and should follow with 8. Nd5, forcing Black to surrender his light-square bishop, 8. . . . Bxd5 9. Bxd5, after which White maintains a small edge.

But it's not uncommon to be tempted by the anti-positional **8. Bxe6?**, leaving Black with doubled e-pawns after **8. . . . fxe6** (Problem 53b), but letting the initiative and superior play pass over to Black.

53b

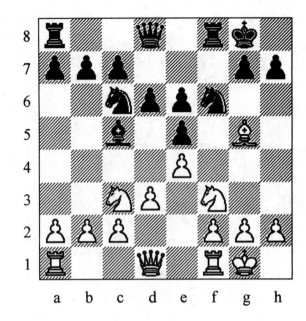

The problem for White here is that Black's doubled e-pawns are quite useful, guarding both d5 and d4. Meanwhile, Black gets an open f-file for his rook, and his queen can sidle into the game by moving to e8 and then out along the e8-h5 diagonal. One should always be saddled with such powerful doubled pawns.

54

It's an easy mistake to make. You pin a piece and take it on the next move, presumably because you derive some advantage, such as winning the exchange (a rook for bishop). But once you've pinned the piece, unless you've missed something, it can't move out of the pin for at least one move, which might enable you to pile up on it and win even more material.

Rx

1. Don't immediately capture pinned units.
2. See if you can win more material by piling on.
3. Especially try to attack pinned units with pawns.
4. In not taking immediately, be sure you haven't missed any saving tactics for your opponent (checks and other nasty threats).
5. In the endgame, maintain a pin to gain a critical tempo.
6. Before taking, let your opponent waste a move trying to get out of the pin.

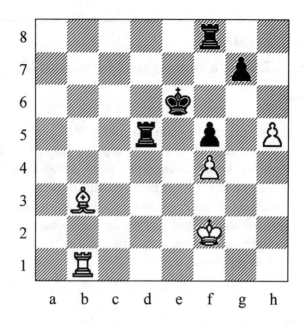

WHITE TO MOVE

White can gain back the exchange here with 1. Bxd5 + ?, but that would be an outright blunder. No need to take the rook, for it's pinned!

What should you do when pinning an enemy piece? Pile up on it, attacking it with additional force. After **Rd1 Rd8 2. Kg3 Rd7** (Black is reduced to making waiting moves) **3. Kh4 Rd6 4. Kg5 Rd8 5. Kg6 Rd7,** White can trade off all the pieces and win the g-pawn, soon making a new queen.

55

Trading and freeing your opponent's game.

When your opponent's position is obstructed by his own forces, he wants to exchange pieces to gain breathing room. If you start trading off pieces, suddenly he's not so cramped and you've lost your advantage.

Rx

1. Don't solve your opponent's problems for him.
2. Avoid trades when your opponent is cramped.
3. Prevent freeing advances.
4. Keep him blocked up and tied down.
5. Use your spatial edge for maneuvering
6. If you are constricted, seek exchanges and unblocking advances.
7. Create diverting counterplay.
8. With a partner or computer, play out blocked-up positions for practice.
9. Alternate taking the superior and inferior sides.

55

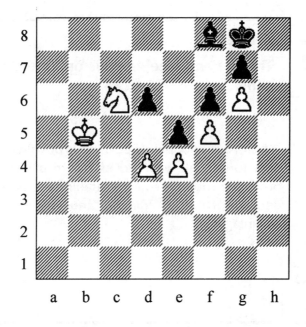

WHITE TO MOVE

White has a big spatial edge here, and he can maximize his greater freedom either by continuing to move in with his king or by advancing the d-pawn. For example, after 1. d5 White will have time to reposition his king to d7 and then occupy e7 with his knight, winning the d-pawn.

Exchanging pawns on e5, however, is a blunder, enabling Black to clear the a3-f8 diagonal, freeing his bishop: **1. dxe5? dxe5,** and Black should draw for sure.

56

Letting your opponent trade off a bad piece.

A typical strategic error is to choose a plan leading to an exchange of an active piece for an inactive or severely limited one. Some openings actually produce bad bishops. The French Defense (1. e4 e6) is a case in point. Black's queen-bishop often has reduced scope, blocked in by its own pawn at e6. White should avoid actions that make it easier for Black to trade this piece.

Rx

1. Let your opponent stew with his own sour bad piece.
2. Avoid trading good pieces for bad, even when it costs you some time.
3. Try to use your superior mobility to acquire other positional advantages, until your opponent surrenders material.
4. Place your pieces so that they have maximum scope.
5. Play to get the good minor piece.
6. Formulate plans taking advantage of this superiority.
7. If you have a bad piece, trade it or improve it by relocating it.

56

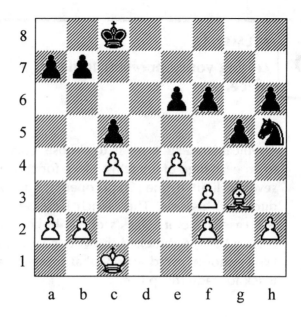

BLACK TO MOVE

In this position, Black might be lured into exchanging knight for bishop, especially if he irrationally follows the principle that bishops are usually slightly better than knights.

But here this is patently not so, for White's bishop can be entombed by **1. . . . e5!,** after which Black will have a tremendous advantage playing with what is tantamount to an extra piece. Imagine Black's knight lodged on d4!

57

Letting your opponent trade off a weakness.

You've mounted the pressure and your opponent has been forced to accept a weak pawn. Direct your pieces at it and the pawn might fall, or the opponent's position may crumble in trying to hold it. Even if he somehow manages to hold, think how hampered and congested his game could be.

But instead, you retreat, and rather than tighten the vice, you advance a restraining pawn, permitting the weakness to be dissolved.

Rx

1. Once you've induced a weak pawn, fix it in place so that the target can't move.
2. Blockade it with a piece and/or guard the square in front of it.
3. Then barrage it with piece attacks.
4. Don't allow its exchange without getting major concessions, such as a powerful gathering assault.
5. Don't trade it. Win it.

57

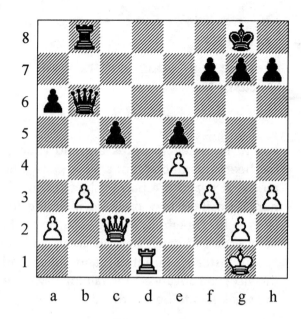

WHITE TO MOVE

White has a splendid game. Black has isolated pawns at a6 and c5, and White's queen and rook are poised to exploit two key open files.

But there's one catch. If White tries to win a pawn by **1. Rd5?**, he allows Black to exchange off his weak c-pawn by advancing it with discovered check, **1. . . . c4+**. After White moves his king to safety, Black rids himself of the albatross by exchanging on b3.

The proper procedure is to first blockade the pawn by placing the queen on c4, or to simply move the king off the a7-g1 diagonal immediately. This avoids future discoveries and enables White to launch a full campaign against Black's infirmities.

58

Automatically taking with check.

It's easy to be taken in by the power of check, especially when you can capture for the same money. But not all checks succeed; some even backfire, as do some captures. The capture of a pawn with the queen, though it gives check, can sometimes be answered by a block that pins the queen to its own king. In other instances, though you get the material with check, you grant your opponent the opportunity to improve his position, such as by forcing him to move his king to a safer spot.

Rx

1. Don't automatically capture just because it's check.
2. Be certain the resulting situation favors you.
3. Consider whether the capture opens lines that can be used against you.
4. Determine if your opponent can answer your check with a threat, preventing you from answering a previous threat.
5. Give it one last look to be sure you haven't missed something.
6. Don't try to do too much.

58

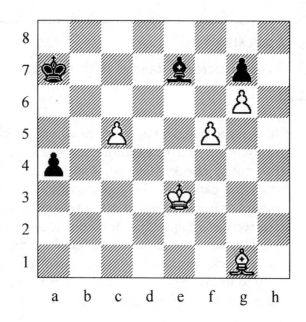

8
7
6
5
4
3
2
1

a b c d e f g h

BLACK TO MOVE

The right plan here is to try to promote the a-pawn, which seems to go through by 1. . . . a3   2. Kd3 Bf6!. If 3. Kc2, then 3. . . . a2 queens; while 3. Bd4 Bxd4+   4. Kxd4 a2 is bad news for White. Nor does throwing in a discovery, 3. c6+ Kb8, change much.

But it's hard not to capture a pawn when you can do so with check. Unfortunately, after **1. . . . Bxc5+?** (putting White's bishop in a skewer) **2. Kd3 Bxg1   3. f6,** White is going to make his own queen, which should at least draw. Checking is often an attempt to justify greed, but it's no excuse for throwing away a win.

AILMENT:

Missing the opportunity to capture with check.

The beauty of capturing with check is that it compels your opponent to answer your move instead of going on with his own plans, such as mating you. If you capture with check, usually you get the next free move and keep the initiative. Often when we see a free pawn, as long as there doesn't seem to be a trap, we take the pawn directly, sometimes oblivious to a better way to do the same thing.

Rx

1. Whenever you can capture, see if you can do it with check.
2. If one of your units is taken, determine if you can insert additional captures with check before finally taking back.
3. Don't capture with check if your opponent can answer with a counterthreat.
4. Consider using checks to gain useful time.
5. Whenever you have a good move, see if you have an ever better one.
6. Look for transpositions to destroy your opponent's plans and to create confusion.

59

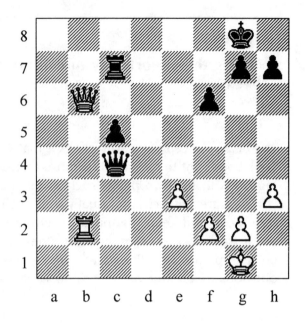

WHITE TO MOVE

White could simply take Black's rook here, 1. Qxc7?, but that gets nowhere after 1. . . . Qc1 +, winning back the rook.

Correct is **1. Qb8 +!,** insuring that Black's rook goes with check on the next move, so that Black never gets the chance to win White's rook.

60

AILMENT:

Surrendering a fianchettoed bishop to win a pawn.

Consider what happens when you fianchetto your king-bishop. First you need two moves to complete the fianchetto. You start by moving the g-pawn, usually one square, which weakens KB3 and KR3. Then you place your bishop at KN2. You'll probably castle kingside. If you give up the bishop, the weaknesses at KB3 and especially KR3 might become pronounced. Imagine an enemy queen ensconced on your KR3, joined by the opponent's knight on your KN4. That's trouble for sure.

Rx

1. Trade off your fianchettoed bishop only for a convincing reason.
2. If you see the possibility of a material gain, carefully analyze the future situation.
3. Decide if you can trade off the bishop, take the pawn, and survive the possible counterattack.
4. If there's any doubt, don't do it.
5. Keep the bishop, and steadily improve your position in other ways.

60

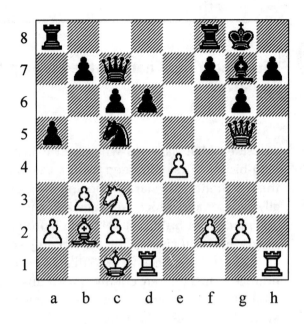

BLACK TO MOVE

Black sees an opportunity to acquire an extra pawn by forsaking his fianchettoed king-bishop. But after **1. . . . Bxc3?   2. Bxc3 Nxe4,** Black's extra pawn means nothing, for now his kingside dark squares are up for grabs.

With **3. Rxh7!,** Black's position falls apart. If 3. . . . Nxg5, Black gets the queen but is done in by 4. Rh8#. Nor does eliminating the queen-bishop fare much better, for 3. . . . Nxc3   4. Qh6 is ruinous.

AILMENT:

Taking the e-pawn at the wrong time.

The wrong time is when your king is still in the center but your opponent is castled. Capturing the enemy e-pawn opens the file for his rook to defile your king (advancing the d-pawn often leads to an exchange of e-pawn for d-pawn). Such rook attacks presage deadly pins and discoveries, and your king might have to flee the barbarians at the gate.

Rx

1. Generally, be super-careful about grabbing the opponent's e-pawn if you're not castled.
2. If you're going to take it, make sure the enemy rooks and queen can't thereafter storm your position.
3. If unsure what to do, just castle and get ready for business.
4. Whenever you're uncertain, try to do something sound and nurturing.
5. After you've secured your position, then look to grab the e-pawn.
6. If your opponent unwisely aims at your e-pawn when he's uncastled, give him a chance to go wrong.
7. Play moves that continue your plans but work against your opponent's.

61

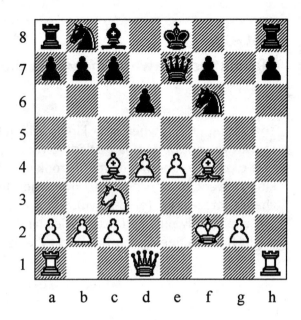

Materially, the two sides are even. However, Black to move can seize the e-pawn with check. But **1. . . . Nxe4+? 2. Nxe4 Qxe4** turns sour after the direct **3. Re1,** pinning Black's queen to his king. It's simply a bad idea to allow the e-file to open with your king still on its original square.

AILMENT:

Fearing to recapture on Q4 with the queen.

We often miss a good queen move because we're afraid of violating the principle against early queen movement. For this reason we don't think to retake on Q4 with our queen, even when there is little danger and the results of not retaking are worse (costs significant material). We also refrain from making strong d-pawn advances when they require the queen's support, thus accepting a passive position.

Rx

1. Don't always dismiss use of the queen in the opening. Chess is not a rigid game.
2. Be flexible. Before beginning a variation that entails bringing out the queen, determine what the consequences are.
3. Try to appreciate whether your centralized queen can be gainfully attacked.
4. Work out whether failure to bring the queen to Q4 will afflict you in other ways.
5. Try to lure your opponent into making attacks hurtful to himself.
6. If your opponent's play surprises you, act natural, but take some time to analyze.

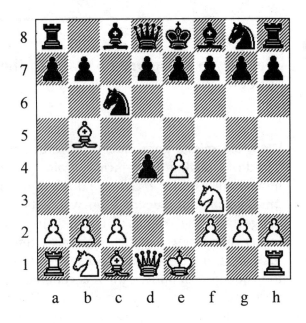

62

BLACK TO MOVE

Diagram 62 is reached after **1. e4 e5   2. Nf3 Nc6   3. d4 exd4   4. Bb5?.** White opts not to take back on d4, fearing that 4. Nxd4 Nxd4?   5. Qxd4 is bad because the white queen is in the center.

Not only is this a wrong evaluation (White's queen sits well on d4 here), but now Black exploits the misplaced b5-bishop by **4. . . . Qa5 +.** Black's pawn at d4, the one White delayed capturing, prevents the bishop from being saved by Nb1-c3.

63

Arbitrarily avoiding a queen trade.

Queen trades are like anything else: they're good or bad depending on circumstances. But some players compulsively say things such as "I need my queen," or "I play well with my queen." Odds are they don't, and that they handle the queen badly and also its two constituent pieces, the rook and the bishop.

Rx

1. Be willing to trade queens for small advantages.
2. Trade queens to keep the enemy king in the center.
3. Trade queens to save valuable time.
4. Don't move the queen frivolously just to avoid an even exchange.
5. Be willing to trade the queen favorably for equivalent material (two rooks, three minor pieces, etc.)
6. Then use the piece combinations supportively to issue double attacks.
7. If you have the queen and your opponent the pieces, look for forking checks and pick them off.

63

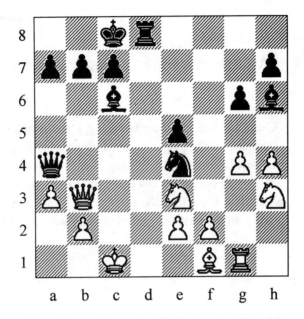

WHITE TO MOVE

This is an example of avoiding a queen trade for no good reason and thereby getting into trouble. White should trade queens to relieve the pressure on his game. For example, after 1. Qxa4 Bxa4 (threatening mate at d1) 2. g5 (breaking the pin on the e3-knight), White might be able to keep things together.

But **1. Qe6+ Bd7 2. Qxe5,** though it retains the queen and steals a pawn, leads to virtual self-mate after **2. . . . Qd1+! 3. Kxd1 Ba4+ 4. Ke1 Rd1+! 5. Nxd1 Bd2#.** White keeps his queen and loses; Black gives his up and wins!

64

Trading only to have less material on the board.

A player who is facing someone he thinks is much stronger might do this, reasoning that the less material there is on the board, the easier it will be to calculate and see threats. It's a strategy employed by a player seeking a draw. Unfortunately, his stronger opponent can use these simplifying exchanges in subtle ways not appreciated by the weaker player to produce sure victory.

Less on the board doesn't necessarily clarify the situation. In fact, with fewer obvious signposts, the inexperienced traveler can get lost.

Rx

1. Be sure to have a reason for every exchange.
2. Don't trade unless it's necessary or leads to an improvement of your position.
3. Don't head for the ending by mechanically trading pieces.
4. If your opponent seeks trades to draw, trick him into making small concessions.
5. Accumulate these concessions and convert them into material gain or a mating attack.

64a

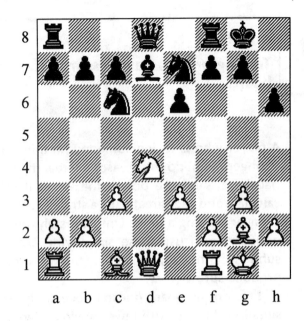

WHITE TO MOVE

The effect of exchanging pieces merely to reduce the amount of material on the board, without regard to the actual circumstances, can be appreciated in Problems 64a and 64b.

In Problem 64a, White should play 1. e4, releasing his queen-bishop, with slightly better chances. The two bishops, a more advanced central pawn, and a somewhat more aggressive position give White a minimal edge.

64b

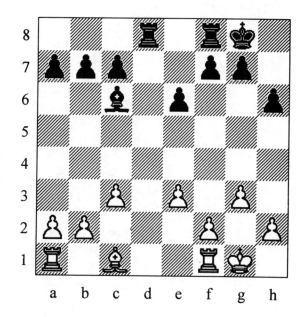

WHITE TO MOVE

But a series of senseless exchanges, **1. Nxc6 Nxc6   2. Bxc6?
Bxc6   3. Qxd8 Rxd8** (Problem 64b), though they don't lose material, actually wind up passing the initiative to Black. Even the
bishops of opposite colors do not guarantee a draw, nor do they
compensate adequately for Black's command of the d-file and
the c6-h1 diagonal. Trading without reference to the needs of a
position is usually a bad idea.

PART • THREE

MISTAKES WITH SPECIFIC UNITS

65

Moving pawns heedlessly.

When you see an enemy piece sitting pretty on a central square, it's natural to want to strike out sharply with a sudden pawn attack. This might seem good if it succeeds in driving the opponent's piece back or out of position. But beware. It could engender weaknesses that won't go away by themselves. You might be saddled with their companion problems for the entire game.

Rx

1. Be extra careful when making aggressive pawn moves.
2. If a pawn move seems unnecessarily risky, don't play it.
3. Empower most attacks with pieces, not pawns.
4. Rely on pawns for stolidity and defense.
5. If not sure what to do, do it with a piece.
6. Sucker your opponent into pushing pawns wildly.
7. Then move in on the weakened squares and get him.

65

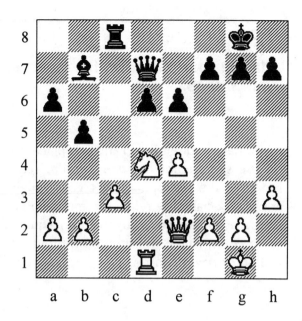

BLACK TO MOVE

The position is approximately even, with each side having offsetting opportunities. Black has use of the c-file, a central pawn majority, and a potentially strong bishop. White can use the d-file and his knight perched in the middle.

It's the placement of the knight that could lure Black into committing the heedless pawn attack, **1. ... e5?**. After **2. Nf5** (attacking the d-pawn) **2. ... Rc6?   3. Qg4,** Black is faced with two serious threats: mate at g7 and the possibility of the knight moving to h6 with check, discovering a winning attack on Black's queen.

66

If you have a lone bishop and you place your pawns on the same color it travels, you're reducing the scope of the bishop. It can't go through its own army, especially the relatively immobile pawns. Besides, by doing so, you abandon squares of the other color, which will then be without satisfactory bishop or pawn control.

Rx

1. Don't block your bishops with your own pawns.
2. Place your pawns on squares of the other color, the one your bishop doesn't use.
3. Achieve harmony by guarding squares of both colors.
4. Place your pawns on the same color only when the situation requires it.
5. Don't put your pawns on the same color out of fear of losing them.
6. Try to fix your opponent's pawns in place so as to block up his bishops.
7. Think of your pieces and pawns as a team. They should complement each other.
8. In bishop endgames, also use your king to guard weakened squares.
9. If you have two bishops, open the game.

66

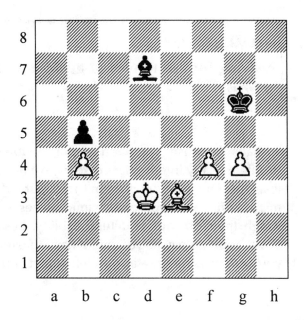

White has two extra pawns, one of which is threatened by Black's bishop. White can safeguard his little ones with 1. g5?, but this throws away his winning chances, for now Black's light-square bishop and king establish an unbreakable blockade on f5.

The way to fight the opposite-color bishop is to place White's pawns on light squares with **1. f5 + !**. This retains White's winning possibilities by combating Black's bishop. Now White's kingside pawns and king can guard the light squares, while his bishop guards the dark squares. It's a perfect team.

AILMENT:

Making foolish moves to avoid doubled pawns.

Perhaps because we learn about doubled-pawn problems early in our chess careers, we never quite lose the fear of having them. Yet doubled pawns might offer all kinds of dynamic pluses that outweigh their obvious structural liability. Besides, to avoid doubled pawns you might have to overextend yourself, causing greater problems than you solve.

Rx

1. Don't be afraid to accept doubled pawns under the right circumstances.
2. When you get doubled pawns, try to utilize the accompanying open lines for attack.
3. Take advantage of any time-gains to add to development.
4. Exploit greater concentrations of pawns in the center.
5. Learn to appreciate compensation. You can accept doubled pawns if what you get as compensation outweighs them in value.

67

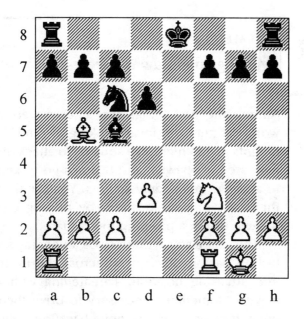

BLACK TO MOVE

Diagram 67 shows what happens when you go out of your way to avoid doubled pawns. Black to move should probably castle. It doesn't matter in which direction, for there is nothing to fear in allowing 2. Bxc6 bxc6, when Black's doubled pawns are not a meaningful factor.

But trying to avoid doubled pawns with **1. . . . Kd7?** drops a piece to **2. d4,** which gains time for the knight-winning advance d5. Black has no satisfactory response.

68

AILMENT:

Moving rook-pawns carelessly.

Among the first things that chessplayers have to worry about are invasive knights and bishops. Knights go to knight-five squares to attack the opponent's c- or f-pawns, and bishops go to knight-five to attack or pin enemy knights. You can try to keep them out of your position by playing either the h-pawn or the a-pawn up one square.

This can also be done once an enemy knight or bishop has already moved across the frontier line into attacking position. Threatening with a rook-pawn is sometimes necessary to drive them back, but often such a pawn move backfires tactically or is simply a waste of time. Even if it seems to succeed, it might inflict damaging weaknesses on your own flank that can eventually be exploited.

Rx

1. Don't move rook-pawns lightly.
2. Determine if you can afford to expend a tempo in this manner, and if the rook-pawn will become a target thereafter.
3. If castled on the same side as the advance, specifically analyze possible enemy sacrifices against the rook-pawn.
4. Also consider the likelihood of line-opening enemy pawn advances.
5. Try to coerce your opponent into unsound or weakening rook-pawn moves.
6. Then open the enemy position to get the king.
7. Use the center to storm across the board to attack a weakened flank.

68

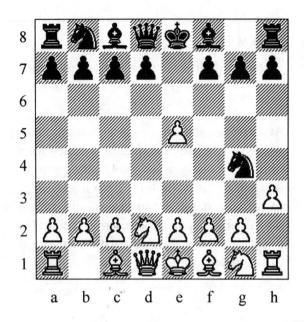

This position was reached after the moves **1. d4 Nf6 2. Nd2 e5 3. dxe5 Ng4.** Black is aiming to get back his pawn, and White should make this a little difficult by developing his king-knight.

But the frivolous rook-pawn move **4. h3?** irreparably weakens g3, allowing the startling **4. . . . Ne3!**, winning the queen, for 5. fxe3 is answered by 5. . . . Qh4+ and mate next.

69

Creating the wrong escape square.

At some point during a game it might be desirable or necessary to provide an escape space for the castled king by moving a pawn. Creating such an escape square, or "making luft," as it is called, is designed to safeguard against the possibility of being mated on the home rank by a queen or rook. The problem is choosing the right luft pawn, for the wrong one can bring trouble.

Rx

1. When castled kingside, usually make luft with the h-pawn.
2. Just be sure the enemy can't guard your KR2.
3. If it seems like he can, consider moving the g-pawn instead.
4. If you make luft with the g-pawn, be certain your king has access to your KN2.
5. If you make luft with the f-pawn, check out potential threats along your QR7-KN1 diagonal.
6. If the endgame is approaching, think about moving your king toward the center instead.
7. Make the luft that incurs the fewest problems.
8. If you commit an error, keep your cool. Don't then make a second mistake.

69

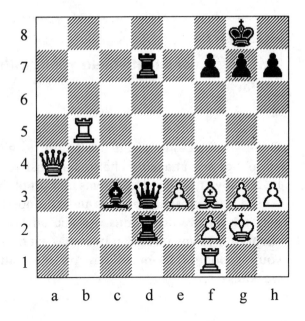

BLACK TO MOVE

White is up a pawn, but the bishops of opposite colors give Black decent drawing chances. One thing to look out for, however, is a back-rank mate, which can be averted by making the appropriate luft (creating an escape hatch for the king).

Black can ward off problems with the safe **1. . . . g6,** when his king can then flee the back rank, unworried about being checked along the a1-h8 diagonal.

But **1. . . . h6?** fails because White's bishop can guard h7. After **2. Rb8+ Rd8 3. Qe8+ Rxe8 4. Rxe8+ Kh7 5. Be4+ Qxe4 6. Rxe4,** White is ahead by the exchange and a pawn, with no immediate difficulties. In this case, making luft by moving the h-pawn is a big mistake.

70

AILMENT:

Moving pawns that shield your castled king.

Once you've castled, you don't want to give your opponent any attacking chances against your king. If you move the shielding pawns in front of the king, you tend to create open avenues and possible targets for enemy operations. As you advance these sheltering pawns farther, it becomes even easier for your opponent to make hay on their attendant weaknesses.

Rx

1. Don't move the pawns in front of your castled king without good reason.
2. Especially be alert when the center is open and your opponent is well developed.
3. This doesn't mean you should never advance such pawns. For example, those moves may be all right if the center is blocked.
4. Also, move pawns in front of your king when tactics dictate it.
5. But be ultra-careful about exposing your king this way.
6. If your opponent exposes his king, open the position and trounce him.
7. Be alert to exceptions. If you see one that you know works for sure, play it instantly and with authority to shock your opponent.

70

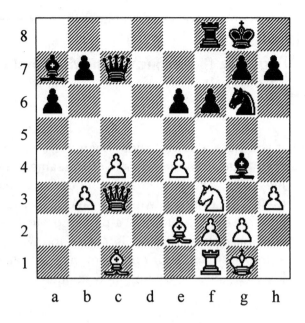

BLACK TO MOVE

This is an equal position, with White having just played **1. h3?**, prodding Black's g4-bishop. This advance, however, weakens White's kingside and actually allows an immediate breakthrough, **1. . . . Bxh3!**.

The point is that **2. gxh3 Qg3 +** (the queen is immune because the f-pawn is pinned). **3. Kh1 Qxh3 + 4. Kg1 Nh4** leaves White virtually helpless because his knight is pinned to his own queen (if 5. Nxh4, then 5. . . . Qxc3).

AILMENT:

Pushing the wrong pawn when mobilizing a majority.

If you have a pawn majority, you have more pawns than your opponent does over the same number of files. Your attacking chances tend to be greater in the sector of this pawn advantage, and you have a good chance to produce a passed pawn, assuming your majority is healthy. But push the wrong pawn at the start, and your opponent may be able to nullify your advantage with timely counters of his own.

Rx

1. When mobilizing a majority, apply Capablanca's rule: push the unopposed pawn first.
2. Don't push the adjacent pawn, for your opponent may be able to hold back your majority.
3. Violate Capablanca's rule only when immediate tactics justify it.
4. Utilize your majority to create a passed pawn.
5. Make a new queen, or use the passed pawn as a decoy to invade on the other side.
6. Advance your majority to develop attacking chances.
7. Generally, attack where you have a concentration of pawns.
8. If you can, immobilize your opponent's majority.

71

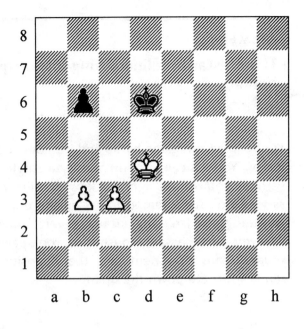

WHITE TO MOVE

White has a winning pawn ending. He should simply start by advancing the unopposed c-pawn (no enemy pawn occupies the same file), maintaining the possibility of generating a useful passed pawn.

A possible conclusion is **1. c4 Kc6   2. b4 Kd6   3. b5 Ke6** (otherwise Black gets outflanked) **4. c5 bxc5 +   5. Kxc5 Kd7   6. Kb6,** crossing over in front of the passed pawn to reach an outside critical square and insuring the win.

But **1. b4?,** throws it all away, for 1. . . . **b5!** shuts down White's pawns and confers the opposition on Black. The game should be drawn.

AILMENT:

Unnecessarily relinquishing a two-square option.

You're in an endgame battle and it's come down to tempi. Your fate is determined by a single move. Perhaps you're in a fight for king dominance, and as you look for a tempo to regain the opposition, you find there isn't any because several moves earlier you unnecessarily pushed a rook-pawn one square. Your opponent gets the opposition and sends your fate down the drain.

Rx

1. Even in innocuous-looking situations, wasting a pawn move can be suicidal.
2. Don't move pawns without definite purpose.
3. Don't advance all your pawns, imagining some final battle, unless you're reasonably sure it's right.
4. Retain at least one unmoved pawn, if circumstances permit.
5. Be certain before moving any pawn, because you can't take it back.
6. In the endgame, use your king to support the advance of your pawns.
7. If you need to gain a tempo, rely on pieces, not pawns.
8. Don't commit yourself to an unclear plan.

72

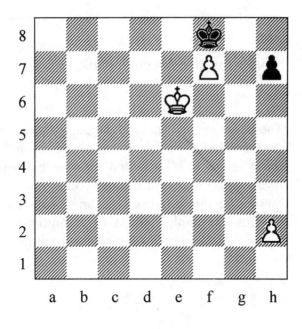

White has an easy win. The correct plan is to stifle Black's king with 1. Kf6!. This forces Black to commit his h-pawn to a movement of one or two squares, after which White will be able to counter correspondingly, moving his own pawn one or two squares—whichever works in the situation.

For example, after 1. Kf6, if 1. . . . h5, then 2. h3 h4   3. Kg6 wins. And if 1. . . . h6, then 2. h4 h5   3. Kg6 also wins.

But what happens if White instead moves his h-pawn at once, **1. h3?.** This is a blunder that, by abandoning the two-square option, throws away the win. Black draws by **1. . . . h6   2. h4 h5   3. Kf6,** and Black is stalemated.

73

Exposing the seventh rank.

The enemy rook is poised dangerously on your second rank, which is the enemy rook's seventh. Everything seems to be guarded for now, but instead of trying to neutralize the rook, you advance a pawn, increasing the length of the line under the rook's control. Suddenly, your king is entombed on its home rank, and it's only a matter of time.

Rx

1. Prevent enemy rooks from occupying your second rank.
2. Once an opposing rook is there, don't open your second rank by moving the wrong pawn.
3. If you must create an escape hatch, keep a pawn back as a shield against the enemy rook.
4. Avoid weakening pawn moves, and don't create any targets.
5. Drive out the enemy rook as soon as you can.
6. Try to place your own rooks on your seventh rank.

73

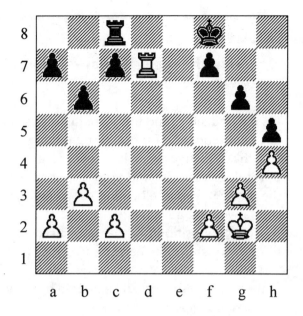

BLACK TO MOVE

Black has to tread very carefully here. White has a ferocious rook on the seventh rank. Black's own rook is at least temporarily tied to the defense of the c-pawn, but fortunately his king can sidle over and drive out the invader with 1. . . . Ke8. Black will then have no problem holding.

But the unprovoked pawn advance **1. . . . f5?** practically throws the game away. With the seventh rank open, White can respond to Kf8-e8 by transferring the rook to h7. Meanwhile, White's own king might be able to infiltrate along the kingside dark squares. The thrust f7-f5? signals a dark day for the black forces.

AILMENT:

Ignoring the oppositional relationship between the kings.

It's the endgame, and there are just kings and pawns left on the board. You do the right thing, you think, and that's to rush your king over to a critical area. But it doesn't work, and your opponent's king gets the better of yours, elbowing its way into your camp with a winning advantage.

The "opposition" is the term used to describe the relationship between the two kings. The kings "stand in opposition" when they are: (1) on squares of the same color, and (2) separated by an odd number of squares along the same line of squares. You "have the opposition" if it is your opponent's move in such a situation. Either your opponent's king must give ground, allowing your king to invade, or his king is unable to penetrate your king's defense, and you hold. If you have the opposition, you have the advantage.

Rx

1. Activate your king in the endgame.
2. Be aware of the oppositional relationship between the two kings.
3. Use the opposition to make inroads or to hold off the enemy king.
4. If you lose the opposition, be alert to the possibility of getting it back meaningfully.
5. Learn all the forms of opposition and study the concept in standard endgame books.
6. Practice playing out pawn endings with kings to familiarize yourself with the opposition's power.

74

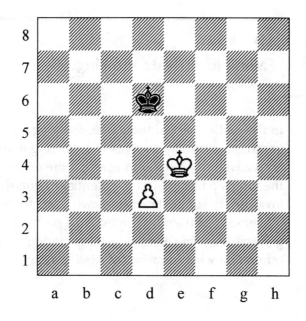

White to play has a forced win in Problem 74, but not by advancing his d-pawn, with the idea that winning is merely a matter of pushing the pawn ahead. For after **1. d4? Ke6   2. d5 + Kd6   3. Kd4 Kd7   4. Kc5 Kc7**, the game should end in a draw.

Instead White should grab the opposition, 1. Kd4!. After Black gives ground, moving to either c6 or e6, White's king advances to the fifth rank. Being two ranks ahead of the pawn, White's king will have little trouble convoying the d-pawn to victory.

AILMENT:

Failing to activate the king.

In the earlier part of the game, the king was endangered, so naturally you castled, tucking it away behind a wall of pawns. But now it's the endgame and the king's participation is essential to guard against invasion, to support certain pawns, and to direct the movement of friendly forces. But, perhaps out of a general fear, you keep the king hidden, while the other side wins because his king is active.

Rx

1. As the endgame starts, move the king back into play.
2. Use the king to support key points and for attack.
3. Most of the time, bring your king toward the middle.
4. A bell should go off once the queens are exchanged. That's when you should consider activating your king.
5. Determine where you'd like to place your king, then get it there.
6. However, make sure to analyze from move to move to avoid walking into a trap.

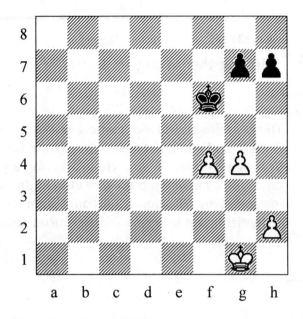

WHITE TO MOVE

White should improve the position of his king. A move like 1. Kf2 serves nicely. But the ill-prepared **1. h4?** throws away White's winning chances. Black strikes back with **1. . . . h5!**, obtaining f5 for his king. A draw is thereby in sight.

AILMENT:

Moving the wrong rook.

This pertains to situations where the rooks are connected, and you must decide which one to move to a particular file. If you choose haphazardly, the other rook might wind up with little to do. In some instances, the ill-fated rook could even become a potential target by virtue of its reduced scope.

Rx

1. Occupy open files with rooks.
2. Once you gain control of a file, try to double rooks.
3. Try to operate with rooks functioning as supportive team members.
4. When either of your rooks can occupy an open or half-open file, figure out how both rooks can be used profitably.
5. If you move the queen-rook to the file, consider what the king-rook will wind up doing.
6. If you muse on moving the king-rook instead, determine how that will affect the queen-rook.
7. Don't move a well-positioned rook without good reason.
8. Choose plans that use both rooks.
9. Never develop one without considering the placement of the other.
10. If you can't decide which rook to move, move the one that allows you to retain the most options.

76

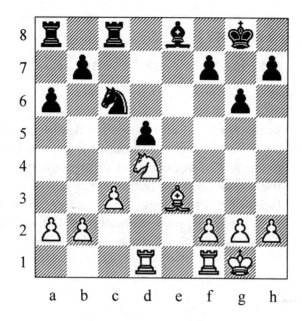

Though there are bishops of opposite colors, White seems to have a little better of it. Black has an isolated d-pawn, Black's bishop, blocked by its own pawns, is inferior to White's, and White is able to seize the d-file with 1. Rfe1.

But by moving the wrong rook to the e-file, **1. Rde1?**, White not only abandons the d-file, he also loses material after **1. . . . Nxd4 2. Bxd4 Bb5.** This solves Black's bad bishop problem in the bargain.

77

AILMENT:

Letting your rook become passive.

Rooks are long-range pieces that work best from far away, on open files and ranks. They tend to be poor defenders. If tied to defense, they might relinquish their attacking ability and be assailed themselves. Especially in the endgame, it's often better to have an active rook and be several pawns down than keep all your pawns but bear a passive rook.

Rx

1. If you see that defending a pawn with a rook keeps you in a hopelessly defensive position, try for rook power by abandoning the pawn.
2. Especially look to occupy the seventh rank or to position your rook aggressively behind enemy passed pawns or on a wide flank.
3. Whenever you have several rook placements that seem to do the job, lean toward the most active one.
4. Just keep thinking: open files, the seventh rank, far away, on the flank, or from behind.
5. If you lose your way, try to think of other rook endings you've had or studied.

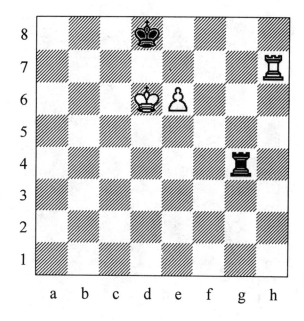

BLACK TO MOVE

White has an extra pawn and is threatening a back-rank mate. Black can draw by keeping his rook active, starting with 1. . . . Rd4+, when 2. Ke5 is answered by 2. . . . Rd1. At that point, Black's aggressive rook insures a series of pesky checks.

But **1. . . . Rg8?,** meekly stopping mate, loses to a queenside rook-shift, **2. Ra7,** threatening a decisive check at a8.

77b

WHITE TO MOVE

The situation here is a little different. Black is threatening to win White's pawn, which should draw.

So White defends his pawns directly by **1. Rd1?**. Though normally you should put your rooks behind passed pawns, here the placement is fairly automatic and even passive. After **1. . . . Kb5 2. d6 Rg8 3. d7 Rd8,** Black will soon move his king into position to win the pawn.

It turns out the more subtle 1. Kc3! is the key to winning, for it immediately allows the rook full cutoff power on the b-file, preventing the black king from crossing over. After 1. . . . Rxd5?, White scores with 2. Kc4!, threatening mate and the rook. Surprisingly, White's king move (1. Kc3!) makes the rook active!

78

Missing the cutoff.

The rook is a strong piece, and if used properly can control a situation. Yours is well placed for the ending, but you forget about its direct-line power and miss the chance to enhance its grip. Your opponent's king moves a file closer, getting close enough to set up a drawing position.

Rx

1. Instead of giving fruitless rook checks, try to cut off the enemy king by placing your rook on a key rank or file.
2. Increase the cutoff whenever possible.
3. Then improve the position of your own king, or advance your own pawn menacingly.
4. Maintain the cutoff for as long as desirable.
5. If you must abandon the cutoff, do so by achieving some of your objectives.
6. If your own king is cut off, break the cutoff and hasten to bring your king back in time.

78

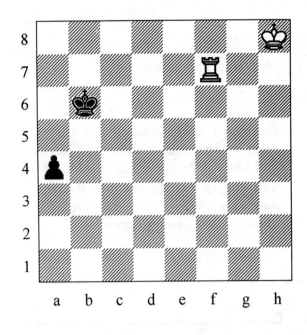

WHITE TO MOVE

This is a sure win for White. By cutting off the enemy king with 1. Rf5!, White will eventually be able to bring his king back and win the pawn. If Black tries to make headway by advancing the a-pawn, White waits until the pawn reaches a3, attacks it with the rook along the third rank, and then overtakes it from behind. For example, White wins after 1. Rf5 a3 2. Rf3 a2 3. Ra3, and the pawn is a goner.

But **1. Kg7?** throws away the win, for now Black's king can enter the fray and protect the pawn: **1. . . . Kc5 2. Ra7 Kb4 3. Kf6 Kb3 4. Ke5 a3 5. Kd4 a2 6. Kd3 Kb2** and draws.

PART FOUR

GENERAL PLAYING ERRORS

79

One of the fastest ways to find trouble is to approach each development as a separate event, independent of all the other moves. Certainly our well-laid plans usually undergo constant modification and revision as the game proceeds, but play aimlessly and nothing is accomplished.

Rx

1. Start a game with certain general ideas.
2. Decide on your opening or defense, and where you want to place your pieces.
3. Think about typical plans.
4. Always try to look three or four general moves ahead.
5. Adapt your plans to the vicissitudes of competition.
6. Don't change your plans without careful analysis.
7. Study well-annotated games by the world's best players, with plenty of descriptive comments.
8. See if you can find similar plans in different games.
9. Try to implement some of these plans in your own games.

79a

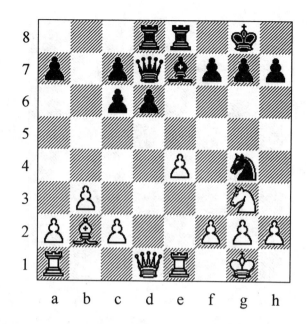

WHITE TO MOVE

This position comes from the second game of the 1908 world championship match between Siegbert Tarrasch (White) and Emanuel Lasker (Black). The beginning moves were **1. e4 e5 2. Nf3 Nc6 3. Bb5 Nf6 4. 0-0 d6 5. d4 Bd7 6. Nc3 Be7 7. Re1 exd4 8. Nxd4 0-0 9. Nxc6 Bxc6 10. Bxc6 bxc6 11. Ne2 Qd7 12. Ng3 Rfe8 13. b3 Rad8 14. Bb2 Ng4** (diagram).

Here White played a combination, winning a pawn: **15. Bxg7! Nxf2 16. Kxf2 Kxg7 17. Nf5+ Kh8 18. Qd4+ f6 19. Qxa7.**

White should now consolidate his forces, exchange down, prevent enemy counterplay, and avoid complications. He should get his pieces to optimal squares, secure his king, and make sure his opponent's pieces don't become active. But somewhere along the line he loses the thread of the game, his play seems to drift aimlessly, and he winds up getting outmaneuvered.

Play continued: **19. . . . Bf8 20. Qd4 Re5 21. Rad1 Rde8 22. Qc3 Qf7 23. Ng3 Bh6 24. Qf3 d5 25. exd5 Be3+ 26. Kf1 cxd5** (Problem 79b).

79b

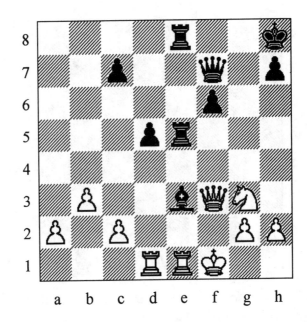

WHITE TO MOVE

Here it's essential that White stop the advance of the f-pawn and get his knight to a more active square. But he played **27. Rd3** (instead of 27. Nf5), and after **27. . . . Qe6**, Black, though down a pawn, is in the driver's seat.

White's final moves were played without much spirit: **28. Re2 f5 29. Rd1 f4** (anchoring in the bishop) **30. Nh1 d4 31. Nf2 Qa6 32. Nd3 Rg5 33. Ra1 Qh6** (it's funny how Black is able to shift from wing to wing at will) **34. Ke1 Qxh2 35. Kd1** (it's too late to run) **Qg1+ 36. Ne1 Rge5 37. Qc6 R5e6 38. Qxc7 R8e7 39. Qd8+** (a meaningless check) **Kg7 40. a4** (this is going nowhere) **f3 41. gxf3** (Problem 79c).

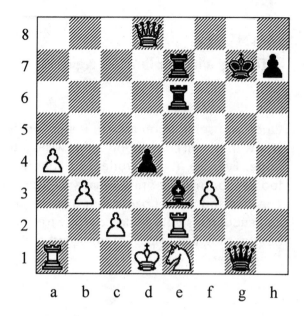

79c

BLACK TO MOVE

White resigned after **41. . . . Bg5,** when it's clear he can't survive much longer. For example, if 42. Rxe6 Rxe6 43. Qc7+ Re7 44. Qa5 Qe3, White has no satisfactory defenses.

80

AILMENT:

Staying with a plan too rigidly.

Once you settle upon a plan, it's generally wise to stay with it until completion, otherwise nothing gets done. Even so, it's imprudent to adhere to a plan too stubbornly, ignoring what's before our eyes. The give and take of battle, our own misjudgments, and sudden insights could call for a fresh approach, but we cling to our past notions and end in a rut.

Rx

1. Yes, play with a plan, but be flexible enough to refashion your thinking from move to move and as situations develop.
2. At the same time, don't whimsically change your aims, but if the position suddenly suggests another outlook, let objectivity guide you.
3. In formulating plans, rely on thorough analysis and cold logic.
4. Evaluate the position before forming a plan.
5. When in a situation you don't understand, look for a common reference point.
6. Once you encounter a new plan in your studies, try to envision how you would put it to good use.
7. Plan to make yourself comfortable and your opponent uncomfortable.

80a

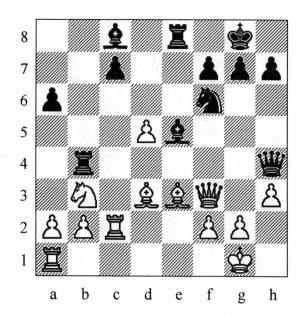

BLACK TO MOVE

In this game, Black's plan has been to attack the enemy king, hoping to crate exploitable weaknesses. And indeed, after **1. . . . Bg4   2. hxg4 Qh2+   3. Kf1 Rxb3** (to remove the guard for a1) **4. axb3 Qh1+   5. Ke2 Qxa1,** it looks like he's doing well.

But the position is in transition, and Black must realize that new conditions necessitate reassessment and possible new plans. He still plays as in the past, however, thinking he has the attack and not appreciating his opponent's counterplay.

The game continued: **6. g5** (driving back Black's knight) **Nd7   7. Bxh7+** (counterplay) **Kxh7   8. Qf5+ Kg8   9. Qxd7 Rb8** (Problem 80b).

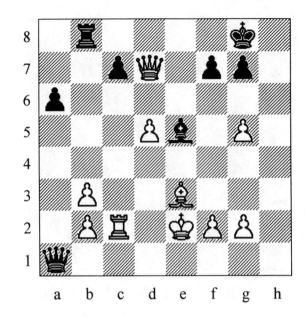

80b

WHITE TO MOVE

The result of Black's plan is a displaced queen. White's attack now broke through: **10. g6! Qh1** (it's too late) **11. Qxf7+ Kh8 12. Qf5 Bd6 13. Rc1 Qh2 14. Rc4 Rf8 15. Qg5 Kg8 16. Rh4 Qe5** (Problem 80c).

80c

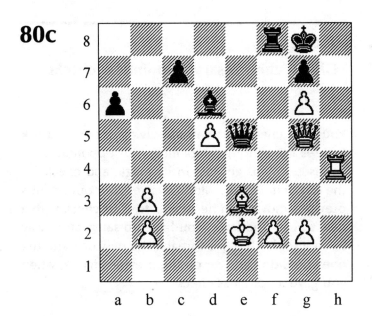

WHITE TO MOVE

It's mate after **17. Rh8+ Kxh8 18. Qh4+** (jettisoning the black queen doesn't help) **Kg8 19. Qh7#.**

81

Giving unnecessary or pointless checks.

You can't checkmate without giving check. A check freezes the action, compelling your opponent's response, so you get lost in its magic and check for the fun of it. But you didn't answer your opponent's previous move, and he replies to your check with a new threat. Suddenly, you have no satisfactory way to counter both of his threats: the new one and the one you didn't answer on the previous move, when you gave a pointless check.

Rx

1. Don't check merely because it's check.
2. Check for the same reason you play any move: because it's a good move.
3. Put yourself in your opponent's place and ask how you would reply to your own check.
4. Don't give a check that winds up wasting time.
5. Don't give a check that forces your opponent to improve his position.
6. Save the check for a rainy day. Catch your opponent without his umbrella.

81

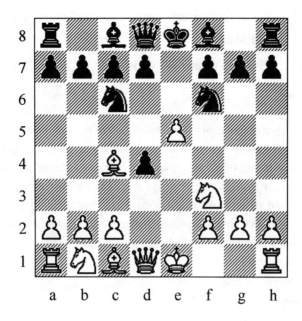

Black's knight is menaced. Rather than move it, Black should counter with **1. . . . d5!**, obtaining a share of the center. But the pointless check **1. . . . Bb4+?** actually loses material. White responds **2. c3,** and after exchanging pawns, **2. . . . dxc3   3. bxc3,** Black will find two of his pieces threatened by small soldiers, with no way to save both.

82

Playing for cheapos.

Some people call this coffeehouse chess. It's not that the perpetrator doesn't play with great skill at times, but he violates principles or takes unnecessary chances, trying to win with flair or by catching an unsuspecting opponent. This looks great when it works, but it often doesn't, for even a weak player could find the refutation accidentally.

Rx

1. Don't play flashy moves to look good.
2. Don't play bad moves because you think your opponent will miss the correct response.
3. Play the board, not the opponent.
4. Don't aim for traps that require you to play a suspect move—unless you are losing, so you might as well.
5. Don't try to win in a few moves, before you've built up your position.
6. In all cases, be objective, logical, and sound.

82

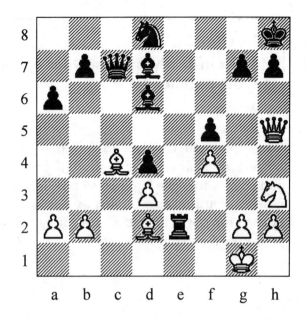

WHITE TO MOVE

White has a clear plan here. He should take Black's rook, 1. Qxe2, with control of several key lines and much the better game.

But getting cute with **1. Ng5?**, hoping for 1. . . . h6 2. Qg6 hxg5 3. Qh5#, allows the unexpected resource **1....** **Rxg2 +! 2. Kxg2 Bc6 + 3. Kg1 g6,** and Black lives, with an extra pawn in his pocket. Good players don't try cheap shots unless absolutely necessary.

83

Your opponent is about to forfeit on time. He's blitzing along attempting to make the time control, and you try to make him overstep by moving just as quickly. You prove to be just as fast as he, but he doesn't run out of time, because you carelessly hang your queen and get mated.

Rx

1. If your opponent is in time trouble, do indeed put the pressure on him, but not by moving as quickly as you can.
2. Answer his threats, but do so with moves that also counterattack.
3. Try to destroy his focus by surprising him with sound but unexpected replies.
4. This might require taking some time, rather than moving instantly.
5. If you're dead lost, look for double attacks. One threat should be obvious, the other subtle. In time trouble, he might miss your hidden point.
6. Don't dwell on the trivial.

83

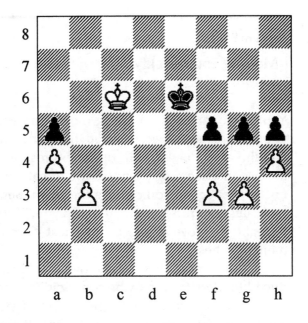

WHITE TO MOVE

Black has just offered a pawn sacrifice. If White had the time, he'd realize that **1. f4** stops all counterplay while keeping out Black's king. White's king could then maneuver freely and win material.

But about to forfeit, White gobbles the offered fruit, **1. hxg5?.** (Whenever you're in time trouble, think twice before accepting your opponent's gifts.) After **1. . . . f4!   2. gxf4 h4,** Black will beat White to the punch and promote first.

84

Moving too quickly.

Your opponent plays a losing move, and you miss your opportunity because you reply instantly. Or you threaten a pawn, your opponent responds with a move that seemingly ignores the threat, and without any reflection you capture the pawn. Suddenly, he issues a surprise shot that mates you. The quick, thoughtless move is one of the most common ailments in chess.

Just remember that every move is crucial. To reduce blunders from moving too rapidly, it helps to keep form, or to follow a specific set of steps on each turn. You should break form only if you have no choice, as for instance when you're running out of time.

Rx

1. After your opponent makes his move, don't analyze it too quickly.
2. First, write it down correctly to start the process. If you don't do this, blanks will appear on your scoresheet that might make you nervous and confused.
3. Then see if your opponent has any obvious threats.
4. Also determine if your opponent's move adequately responds to your previous move.
5. If it seems to ignore your previous move, ascertain if it's concealing some tricky answer.
6. Make sure he has no surprise checks, captures, or threats.

7. Only after you've thoroughly analyzed the situation should you begin the process of deciding your next move.
8. Remember, the best defenses are those that seem to ignore your opponent's threats.

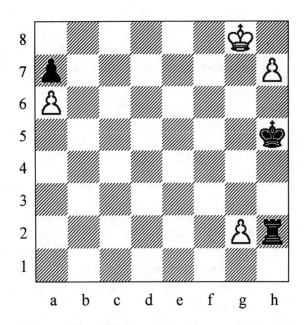

BLACK TO MOVE

Black moves impulsively with the natural **1. . . . Rxg2 + ?**, which actually loses after **2. Kf8 Rf2 + 3. Ke8 Re2 + 4. Kd8 Rd2 + 5. Kc8 Rc2 + 6. Kb8 Rb2 + 7. Kxa7** (or 7. Ka8), and the checks end.

If he took some time to analyze the situation (assuming he has the time), Black should instead play 1. . . . Kg4!, when 2. h8/Q Rxh8 + 3. Kxh8 Kg3 4. Kg7 Kxg2 will eventually draw. The drawing idea is that after White's king captures on a7, Black's king must move to c7.

AILMENT:

Unnecessarily putting your pieces in pins.

This usually happens when you block a check. Obviously, you'll avoid an interposition if you see it loses material. A problem arises when material is not immediately lost. If you could get out of the pin shortly thereafter, say by castling, putting yourself in a pin might be okay. But there are other instances where the pin can't be satisfactorily broken, and the pinned unit becomes a real target, piled on and won.

Rx

1. Avoid getting caught in a pin unless it's clearly desirable or necessary.
2. If castled, try to get out of check by moving the king to a safe square (the corner).
3. If uncastled, try to block the enemy check with a time-gaining move.
4. Stick a pawn in the enemy piece's face.
5. If you must accept being in a pin, don't linger in it for too long.
6. If uncastled and in a pin, try to end it satisfactorily by castling.
7. Don't play Russian roulette with your chess positions.

85

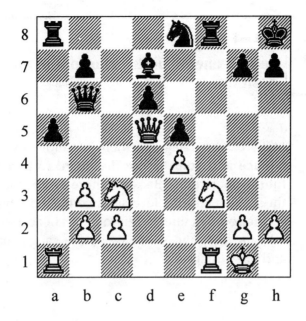

White is in check. He should simply slide his king to the corner and proceed with his game. But blocking the check by putting the rook in a pin, **1. Rf2?,** is a violation of principle that costs at least the exchange. After **1. . . . Nf6,** White cannot save his queen and also prevent Black from moving his knight to g4.

86

AILMENT:

Letting enemy units camp out in your position.

Many players telegraph their intentions by moving a piece into your half of the board to prepare for future operations. Because there is no immediate threat, you let the piece sit uncontested. This gives your opponent time to reinforce his beachhead with other forces, and suddenly you're caught napping and are besieged.

Rx

1. Don't let enemy pieces sit in your half of the board.
2. Especially watch out for skulking knights.
3. If the situation permits, play P-R3 and drive back the intruder.
4. Make sure you can survive the weakness of this advance.
5. Don't make unnecessary defensive moves.
6. Be psychologically prepared for surprise invasions.
7. If you're hit with an unexpected move in the opening, keep or fight for the initiative.
8. Be willing to accept a problem for a greater good.

86a

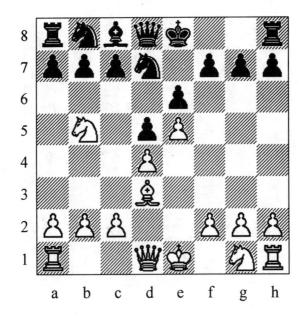

This position comes about after the opening moves **1. e4 e6 2. d4 d5 3. Nc3 Nf6 4. Bg5 Be7 5. e5 Nfd7 6. Bxe7 Qxe7 7. Nb5 Qd8 8. Bd3** (diagram).

Black shouldn't allow White's knight to sit in the heart of his position. With **8. . . . a6**, he could compel it to withdraw. Instead, Black tried to dislodge the intruder with **8. . . . c6?**, but that only invites it to visit longer. After **9. Nd6+ Ke7 10. Qh5 g6 11. Qh4+ f6 12. Nh3 Na6 13. Nf4 g5?**, the game Speyer-Couvee reached the following position (Problem 86b).

86b

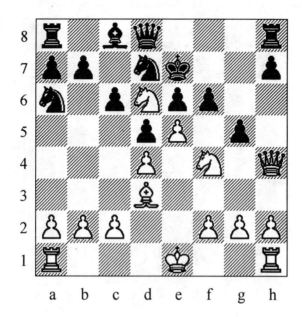

WHITE TO MOVE

Combat concluded with **14. Qxh7 + ! Rxh7   15. Ng6#!**. In the final setup, White's knights could give Black's position as their home address.

86c

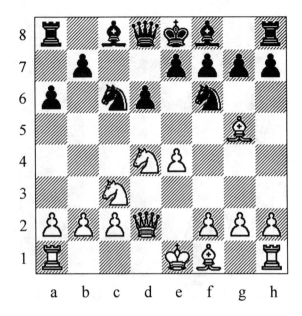

BLACK TO MOVE

This diagram develops from a Sicilian Defense after **1. e4 c5   2. Nf3 Nc6   3. d4 cxd4   4. Nxd4 Nf6   5. Nc3 d6   6. Bg5 a6   7. Qd2.**

Black has several reasonable moves at his disposal here, but he chooses the unnecessary retreat **7. . . .Nd7?**. This allows White's knights to enjoy Black's playground: **8. Be2 g6** (the line **8. . . . h6?   9. Ne6 fxe6   10. Qh5+ g6   11. Qxg6** mate is most amusing) **9. Nd5** (note that 8. . . . e6, to drive away the d5-knight, is unplayable because of the pin) **f6   10. Ne6 Qa5   11. Ndc7+ Kf7   12. Nd8+ Kg7   13. Ne8+,** and Black resigns (Problem 86d).

86d

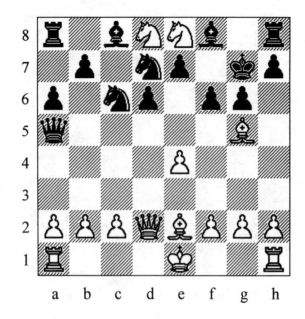

In this final situation, White's knights have assumed honored positions in Black's homeland. If the king retreats to g8, White's bishop signals the end by checking on c4.

AILMENT:

Relying on a vulnerable unit.

If a defending unit can be captured, it's not really defending. This holds too if the guarding unit can be driven away or rendered immobile, either by being pinned or tactically overburdened. Sometimes if a defense works on one move, it lulls us to think that it will hold on the next.

Rx

1. Don't put your hopes on a capturable, pinnable, or chaseable backup.
2. Don't assume a defense works now because it worked before.
3. Add useful protection whenever feasible.
4. Don't let your pieces stay under attack unnecessarily.
5. If you decide to move the threatened piece out of attack, do so with a gain of time.
6. Always try to have bolstering variations and contingencies.
7. When analyzing positions, do it twice: once attacking, once defending.

87

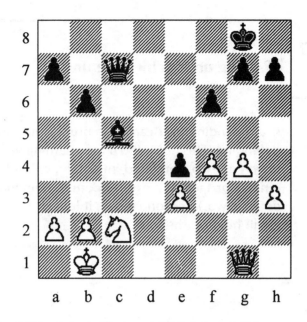

BLACK TO MOVE

Can Black win a pawn here? After all, his bishop pins the e3-pawn to White's queen, so f4 is apparently unguarded. But **1. . . . Qxf4?** is erroneous because it relies on a faulty pin, which is refuted by **2. b4!.** Black's bishop will soon be extinct.

88

AILMENT:

Self-trapping your own pieces.

You see a chance to take a rook-pawn with your bishop. You do so, and your opponent advances the knight-pawn, trapping your bishop. How do you get out? You probably don't, and the bishop falls in a few moves. Or your knight is attacked, and you advance it into enemy territory, safely for now, but where it's eventually gobbled by enemy forces.

Rx

1. Don't be greedy.
2. Don't move unnecessarily quickly.
3. Don't take unprotected units without first reconnoitering for possible traps.
4. If you're considering taking a rook-pawn with a bishop, make sure the piece can't be sealed in after the capture.
5. If you're thinking about moving a knight into enemy territory, certify that the piece is secure and can get out of the lion's den.
6. Take an extra minute or two to be certain.

88

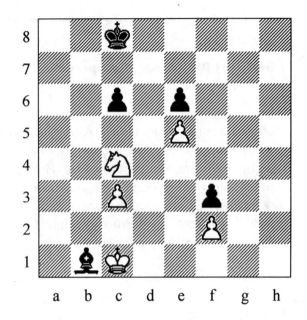

BLACK TO MOVE

Black should withdraw his bishop to safety and not be lured into **1. . . . Ba2?,** for after **2. Nd6+ Kd7 3. Kb2,** Black has no better move than **3. . . . Bd5.** But the bishop is trapped and netted by **4. c4.** Black has self-trapped his own bishop.

89

Holding on to material unreasonably.

Let's say you're ahead by three pawns but are facing a tremendous onslaught. By allowing your opponent to win back one or two pawns, you'd still be ahead, and his attack would be broken. But greed wins out: you cling to your material and get mated.

Rx

1. Be willing to surrender some of your material advantage to defuse your opponent's assault.
2. Convert your material plus into a winning attack.
3. Don't try to hold on to material unreasonably.
4. Use your material edge to control the flow of events.
5. If you're having trouble simplifying, seek out a specialist for advice.
6. Study the games of Capablanca and Fischer.
7. Whenever you want to develop some aspect of your play, study the games of a great player known for expertise in that area.

89

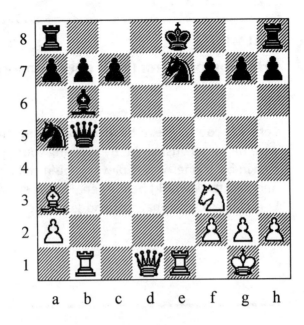

BLACK TO MOVE

This position comes from an 1849 game between Paul Morphy (White) and his father, Alonzo Morphy. Black is ahead by a piece, but he should probably give up his queen to stop White's assault. For example, 1. . . . Qd7 2. Rxe7+ Qxe7 3. Bxe7 Kxe7 would at least prolong the game.

But Black tried to keep his queen, **1. . . . Qa6?,** and White's attack proceeded merrily along: **2. Rxe7+ Kf8 3. Qd5 Qc4 4. Rxf7+ Kg8 5. Rf8#.**

This tends to be a late-middlegame to endgame problem. It occurs after you already have the big material advantage of an extra queen. Instead of using the extra queen to force a quick mate, you want the security of making another queen, thinking it will win faster. But remarkably, the presence of the second queen gives the other player a gold mine of opportunities. He forcibly ditches his remaining material, leaving himself without a legal move, and he draws by stalemate—thus proving the adage that less can be more.

Rx

1. Make sure you know how to mate with an extra queen.
2. Once you get ahead by a queen, play for mate.
3. Don't try to promote other pawns into unnecessary queens. One extra queen should do it.
4. Don't bother trying to win irrelevant pawns.
5. Once up by a queen, don't worry over trivialities.
6. Don't allow the game to go on longer than it should. Just get it over with.
7. Always analyze your games after playing them so that you can focus on your recurring problems.

90

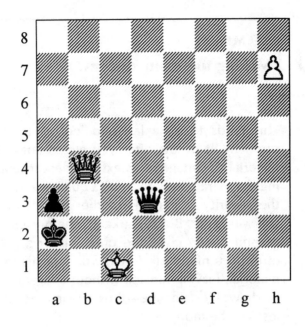

WHITE TO MOVE

White to play has an elementary win. He should simplify by checking on d2. After the trade of queens, White promotes first and has the time to stop Black's pawn.

But the careless **1. h8/Q?,** allows Black to ditch his queen, producing stalemate, **1. . . . Qc2 + !** (or 1. . . . Qd1 + !). After the queen is captured, Black is left without a move.

91

AILMENT:

Grabbing pawns.

Everyone has committed this infraction. We see a chance to take a pawn, it appears we can get away with it, so we pounce. Often it winds up costing too much time or there's a costly refutation.

Rx

1. Don't seize "free" pawns immediately.
2. Be sure you haven't overlooked a subtle defense.
3. Also determine whether taking the pawn distracts you from other requirements.
4. Be certain your king is not suddenly endangered.
5. Especially be on the lookout for nasty checks that could overturn an intricate variation.
6. If you can play a strong move that ignores taking the pawn, seriously ponder it.
7. Develop a sixth sense.

91

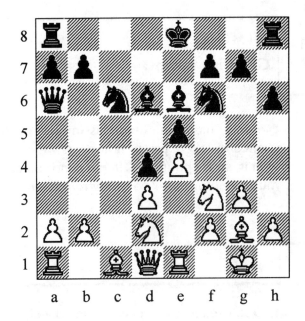

BLACK TO MOVE

Black can capture White's d-pawn with his queen, **1....
Qxd3?,** but that's the criminal act of pawn-grabbing. The retreat
(actually, the advance backward) **2. Bf1** punishes the transgres-
sion by trapping the queen.

92

Taking unnecessary material.

You're ahead by a queen. You start tinkering with her highness, trying to nickel-and-dime your opponent for pawns. You gain some insignificant units in the process, but overlook a back-rank mate. It's a problem as common as air.

Rx

1. Once you get overwhelmingly ahead in material and have a "sure win," take absolutely no chances.
2. Don't go out of your way to win a paltry pawn.
3. Especially avoid overuse of the queen.
4. Simplify ruthlessly, and don't lose sight of the game's real object, playing for mate.

92

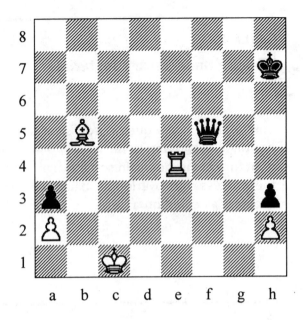

BLACK TO MOVE

Black in command should simply collect the bishop, 1. . . . Qxb5, which will lead to further gains shortly. But instead he goes for the big enchilada—the rook—with **1. . . . Qxe4?,** and is hit with **2. Bd3!,** when 2. . . . Qxd3 is stalemate.

93

Sacrificing without good reason.

There are two types of sacrifices: sham ones and true ones. In a sham or pseudo sacrifice—the most common kind—a favorable outcome can be foreseen, so it's no sacrifice at all. With a true sacrifice, the consequences are not entirely clear, so there is an element of risk. You might get into the habit of making the latter type. Though you'll startle most players at first, you'll probably lose in the end, for if there's no obvious justification for a sacrifice, the chances are good that the defender will find a refutation. After all, he has no choice but to defend himself.

Rx

1. Sacrifice only with a definite reason.
2. Consider a sacrifice if your opponent has played badly and you have a powerful position.
3. Calculate the sacrifice carefully and deeply.
4. If you can't see a positive and sure result to the offering, don't take the risk.
5. Don't take unnecessary chances just because you're facing a weaker player.
6. The only times you should consider sacrificing without certainty are when you're losing anyway or when you're in a must-win situation.
7. If your opponent plays a suspicious-looking sacrifice, look extra hard to find a refutation.

93

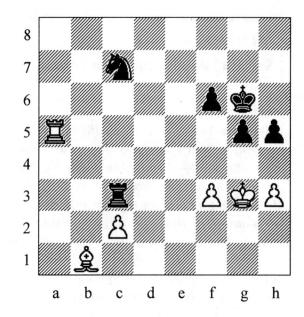

Material is even, but White has a bishop for a knight, which might explain White's desire to activate his bishop, **1. Ba2?,** sacrificing the c-pawn, **1. . . . Rxc2.**

White's hidden trick is **2. Bb1,** pinning the rook to its king. Black's even trickier resource is **2. . . . h4+   3. Kg4 f5+!,** when **4. Rxf5** is answered by **4. . . . Rg2#!.**

94

Declining a refutable sacrifice out of fear.

You're suddenly stopped in your tracks by a bolt from the blue. In trying to analyze it, you can't see why you shouldn't capture the offered unit. You conclude, however, that you must be wrong, that you must be missing something, either because your opponent is too good or because he is too confident. You wind up not taking the piece, and lose because the sacrificial offering remained on the board.

Rx

1. If your opponent offers you a piece, by all means see if there's a definite problem with its capture.
2. If there is, don't accept it.
3. But if investigating the circumstances closely doesn't uncloak a stinger, take the sacrifice.
4. Place the burden of proof on your opponent.
5. If you don't accept an unsound sacrifice, you're allowing your opponent to get away scot-free with whatever damage he's inflicted.
6. Don't be intimidated by brash play. Show your mettle. Take the material, rebuff the intruder, and go for the kill.

94

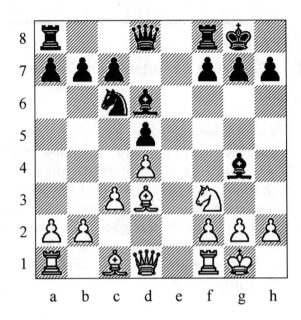

WHITE TO MOVE

White thinks he sees an unpinning combination beginning with **1. Bxh7 + ?.** The idea is that taking the bishop runs into a knight check on g5, uncovering an attack on the g4-bishop by White's queen. So Black declines the h7-bishop out of fear of being checked. He plays **1. . . . Kh8?.**

The best way to refute an unsound sacrifice is to accept it. After **1. . . . Kxh7 2. Ng5 + Qxg5!,** Black has disciplined White's inexactitude, for both queens are hanging. However White responds, he loses at least a piece.

95

AILMENT:

Falling into stalemate.

You're well ahead, but you get lazy about forcing checkmate. You become sidetracked and mindlessly try to capture the remnants of your opponent's army. In the process you walk into stalemate.

Rx

1. Once you have a material advantage that insures a win, simplify in order to reduce enemy counterplay.
2. If you have an extra piece, play for mate or make a new queen and then play for mate.
3. When you're closing in on a materially deficient defender, don't seize his last pawn, leaving him without a move.
4. When your opponent has a little, and you have a lot, be especially sensitive to the pitfall of stalemate.

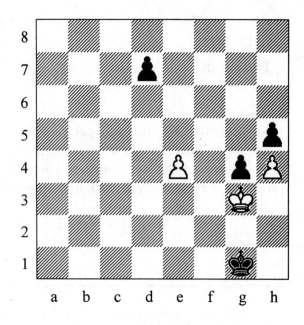

BLACK TO MOVE

Black is up a pawn, and if he merely shifts his king between g1 and h1, eventually White's king must give ground. Black's king moves to h2 and escorts the g-pawn to queendom.

But the overly defensive **1. . . . d6?,** misguidedly trying to stop White's e-pawn from moving, flings it all away. White can advance anyhow, **2. e5!,** Black has to capture, **2. . . . dxe5,** and that's stalemate.

96

AILMENT:

Allowing unnecessary counterplay.

You have a winning game, but you need to coordinate your pieces. You could get a handle on the position, but you avoid a few simplifying exchanges, the situation complicates, and you blunder into mate.

Rx

1. Winning a chess game is not always a matter of bravado.
2. If you want to win smoothly, think about minimizing enemy counterattacks and making your job easier.
3. When you get ahead, simplify—plain and simple.
4. Try to trade pieces.
5. Complete your development.
6. Avoid taking unnecessary risks and safeguard your king.
7. Maintain control of key squares and lines.
8. Keep your goal—mate—in mind at all times.
9. Develop your own approach to decision-making. Master it.

96

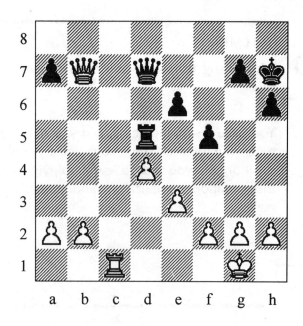

WHITE TO MOVE

White is a pawn ahead, and with the exchange of queens, 1. Qxd7 Rxd7, retains capital chances to win the endgame.

But the overzealous **1. Rc7?,** seemingly winning because of the skewer to queen and g-pawn, allows the countershot **1.... Rc5!.** If White takes Black's queen, Black mates at c1. Taking the c5-rook with the d-pawn walks into mate at d1. Finally, taking Black's rook with White's loses the white queen. White's failure to simplify therefore costs him a rook.

97

AILMENT:

Failing to encourage your opponent to go wrong.

Your opponent makes a threatening move, positioning one of his units to capture one of yours. Without thinking very much, you respond with a defensive backup. But it turns out you didn't have to defend your attacked unit, for if your opponent took it, he would have given you a devastating counter. You moved too fast and lost your chance to trap the enemy.

Rx

1. Don't do the unnecessary.
2. When one of your units is attacked, see how to safeguard it, but also determine if the threat is really that at all.
3. Ask yourself what happens if you let it be captured.
4. Determine if your opponent will then be out of position and vulnerable elsewhere.
5. Give your opponent enough rope to hang himself.
6. Get into the habit of asking "what if" questions.
7. If you see a good move that doesn't win, save it for the right time.

97

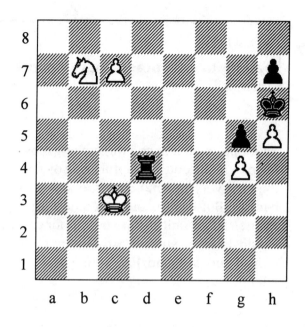

BLACK TO MOVE

Black seems lost, and the perfunctory 1. . . . Rd1, trying to get behind the passed pawn, indeed loses to the interposing 2. Nc5!.

He should instead give his opponent a chance to go wrong with **1. . . . Rd7,** the most practical try. If White then blithely makes a new queen, **2. c8/Q?,** Black saves the day with **2. . . . Rc7+! 3. Qxc7** stalemate!

White can win after 1. . . . Rd7, however. The key move is 2. Nd6!, when 2. . . . Rxc7+ 3. Kb4 leaves White threatening Nd6-f5 mate, and 3. . . . Kg7 fails to 4. Ne8+, forking king and rook. But since Black is lost anyway, he might as well try something tricky.

98

Missing the chance to cut your losses.

Your piece is trapped and you must lose something. When the shock wears off, you're down three points worth of material with no compensation. Suddenly you realize that you've overlooked an opportunity to complicate the game and put up greater resistance.

Rx

1. When a piece of yours is trapped, try to sell its life dearly, capturing as much as you can for it.
2. See if you can turn its loss around, sacrificing it to rip open the enemy king's position or to give your opponent a problem or two.
3. Can you ruin his pawn structure, prevent his king from castling, or force him to lose valuable time?
4. Don't give up on a position just because you can't find the answer. If you think you're right, look a little longer and harder.
5. Try to turn the problem into the solution.

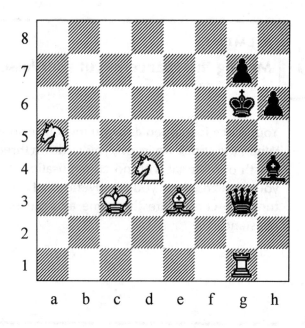

BLACK TO MOVE

Black has just walked into a pin and must lose his queen. But rather than the passive 1. . . . Kh7?, fleeing to safety while only getting a rook for his queen (2. Rxg3 Bxg3), Black should sell the queen's life dearly with the active **1. . . . Qxg1! 2. Bxg1 Be1+ 3. Kd3 Bxa5.** With a bishop and two connected pawns for White's two pieces, Black should at least draw. If you have to lose material, lose as little as possible.

99

AILMENT:
Missing a saving possibility.

It's so easy to give up hope. You're down a lot of material, your position's in a shambles, mate seems inexorable. Indeed, your opponent seems to be quite confident. This is the time you should be looking for a swindle. But you don't. You play on dispiritedly and lose without any resistance.

Rx

1. When you have a lost game, certainly look for counterchances.
2. If you can't find any, at least investigate ways to save the game by drawing.
3. Imagine stalemate possibilities, then proceed to create the necessary conditions for them.
4. Look to trade off, producing a situation with insufficient mating material.
5. If behind by a pawn or two, try to fashion an ending with bishops of opposite color.
6. If conceivable, try to establish a fortress.
7. There's an optimal strategy for every situation, even losing ones, and finding it is an essential part of the play. Find yours.

99

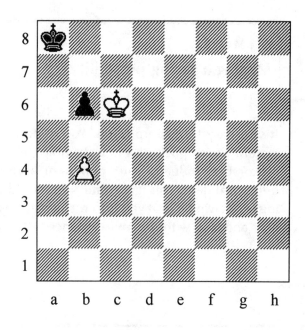

BLACK TO MOVE

Here's the situation: Black's pawn is attacked. If he defends it with **1. . . . Ka7?**, the advance **2. b5** wins the pawn and shortly thereafter the game. A possible conclusion is **2. . . . Ka8   3. Kxb6 Kb8   4. Ka6 Ka8   5. b6 Kb8   6. b7 Kc7   7. Ka7**, and it's all over.

But if Black realizes the pawn is lost no matter what, he might find that **1. . . . b5!** is a better way to lose it. After **2. Kxb5**, Black gets a meaningful opposition with **2. . . . Kb7** and the game is drawn.

100

AILMENT:

Resigning prematurely.

Experienced players know that there's often a chance for a last-minute knockout, even in the worst-played games. A player can have the edge for 30 moves, blunder on the 31st move, and get mated.

Just keep on fighting. Try a last-ditch something. It might work. I have seen probably dozens of games where the resigner really had a forced win.

Rx

1. Once you get a losing game, look for unexpected tactics, offer stout resistance, create sucker punches, fight tooth and nail.
2. Take advantage of your opponent's complacency.
3. Do your best to boil up some counterplay.
4. Psych yourself up.
5. Look determined.
6. Manifest resolve to fight to the death.
7. To change the result, change your attitude.
8. Take everything you've just read with a grain of salt.

100

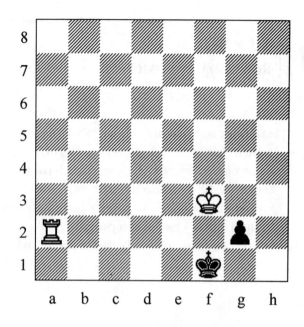

BLACK RESIGNS

White has just played Ke4-f3 and looks to be winning, for promoting the g-pawn to a queen loses to a mating check at a1. But the obituary notice is somewhat premature, for underpromoting to a knight, **1. . . . g1/N+!,** saves the day because of the check. If Black is careful thereafter, he should hold.

Tactics Glossary

ATTRACTION The forcing of a defending unit to an exploitable square.

BACK-RANK MATE A mate given by a queen or rook along the first or eighth rank.

BATTERY Two pieces of the same color attacking along the same line supportively.

CHECK A direct attack to the king.

CHECKMATE The situation of having no legal move when the king is in check. The end of the game.

COMBINATION A forced series of moves, usually involving sacrifice and often merging several tactical themes, which leads to a definite improvement in position.

CORRIDOR MATE A mate by a queen or rook along a rank or file.

COUNTERATTACK Usually, answering your opponent's threats with threats of your own.

DECOY A stratagem that lures an enemy unit to an area or a particular square.

DEFLECTION The forcing of a defending unit from its post.

DESPERADO A threatened or trapped piece sacrificed for the most it can get or to inflict damage.

DIRECT ATTACK Moving a unit into position to capture another with advantage.

DISCOVERY An attack by a stationary piece unveiled when a friendly unit moves out of its way.

DOUBLE CHECK A discovery in which both the moving and stationary units give check.

DOUBLE THREAT Two separate threats, not necessarily made by the same unit.

EN PRISE   Referring to a unit that is attacked and undefended.

FORK   An attack by one unit against two or more different enemy units at the same time.

GAMBIT   A voluntary sacrifice, usually of a pawn in the opening.

IN-BETWEEN MOVE   See *zwischenzug*.

INTERFERENCE   Cutting the power of an enemy unit by putting a unit in the way, often with a time-gaining attack.

JETTISON   Forcing your opponent to sacrifice material to save the king or avoid loss of even greater material.

KING HUNT   A series of moves that chase the enemy king all over the board until it is mated.

KINGSIDE ATTACK   A general campaign against an opponent's king castled on the kingside.

MATING ATTACK   A general onslaught against the king, resulting in mate or material gain.

MATING NET   A forced mate.

OVERLOAD   A situation in which a unit cannot fulfill all its defensive commitments.

PILING ON   Exploiting a pinned unit.

PIN   An attack on an enemy unit that shields a more valuable unit.

PIN OVERLOAD   Exploiting an overloaded unit by pinning it.

PROMOTION   Advancing a pawn to its last rank and converting it into a queen, rook, bishop, or knight.

REMOVING THE DEFENDER   The same as undermining.

REMOVING THE GUARD   Another name for undermining.

SACRIFICE   The offer of material for some other kind of advantage, such as time.

SAVING   Avoiding the loss of material, usually with a time-gaining threat.

SHUT-OFF   A line block that prevents an enemy unit from controlling or using a rank, file, or diagonal.

SKEWER   An attack on an important unit that by moving exposes another unit to capture.

SMOTHERED MATE A mate by a knight in which the losing king's escape squares are all blocked by its own forces.

STALEMATE A drawn game. The situation of having no legal move but not being in check.

STRATEGY A general plan. The opposite of tactics.

SUPPORT MATE A mate given by a unit that is protected by another.

TACTICS Immediate attacks and threats. The opposite of strategy.

TECHNIQUE Getting the most out of a position by precise maneuvering, with attention to nuances and subtle moves.

TRAPPED PIECE A piece with no escape that can be attacked and captured, usually with advantage.

TRAPPING Winning a unit that has no escape, usually by attacking it with less valuable units.

UNDERMINING Capturing or driving away a unit that guards another.

UNDERPROMOTION Promoting a pawn to a rook, bishop, or knight, but not to a queen.

UNPIN A counterattack that breaks a pin, gains time to break a pin, or ends a pin by eliminating or diverting a pinning unit.

WINNING THE EXCHANGE Gaining a rook for a bishop or knight.

X-RAY Two friendly pieces supporting each other for defense or attack along the same line, separated from each other by an enemy piece of the same power.

ZUGZWANG A situation in which moving worsens your position.

ZWISCHENZUG An unexpected move or surprise finesse played before completing an anticipated response, such as an obvious recapture.

Tactics Index

(Numbers refer to diagrams)

Bishop Sacrifice	5	8d	11b	12	17	18	23	39
	40	58	70	92	94	(13)		
Breakthrough	28d	(1)						
Center Pawn Roller	9	(1)						
Discovery	7b	27	32a	57	82	(5)		
Double Threat	65	77b	81	87	(4)			
Fork	6a	10	12	14a	14b	14c	29b	30b
	35a	35b	36	42	59	62	69	79a
	97	(17)						
Gaining Time	13b	30a	34a	34b	34c	(5)		
Knight Sacrifice	1	7b	14a	14b	14c	15	32a	50
	68	(9)						
Mating Attack	1	5	6b	8b	11a	15	17	19
	20b	21	23	41	51	68	70	89
	(16)							
Mating Net	11b	22	27	38	48b	60	63	80c
	86b	86d	(10)					
Multiple Threats	8d	(1)						
Opposition	37	71	74	(3)				
Overload	32b	(1)						
Pin	6c	6d	25	33	35a	43	45	54
	61	67	85	94	96	(13)		
Promotion	46	52b	58	72	83	84	99	100
	(8)							
Queen Sacrifice	6b	8b	20b	21	22	38	52b	60
	63	69	86b	87	90	94	96	(15)
Rook Sacrifice	19	21	27	28d	29b	30b	45	60
	80c	82	96	97	(12)			

Simplification	39	40	(2)				
Skewer	7a	18	26a	26b	47	77a	98	(7)
Stalemate	45	90	92	95	(4)		
Trapping	76	88	91	(3)			
Undermining	32c	50	75	(3)			
Unguarding	24	(1)					
Unpin	93	(1)					

Sacrifice Squares

(Examples refer to diagram numbers)

Squares	Examples			
b4	8d	39		
b8	21			
c2	90			
c5	96			
c6	22	29b		
c7	97			
d1	38	63		
d3	92			
d4	28d	50		
d7	21	96		
e3	45	68		
e4	6b	14a	32a	
e5	14b	14c	52b	
e6	19			
e8	69			
f2	5	15	12	30b
f4	8b	18	87	
f5	20b			
f7	1			
g1	58			
g2	82			
g3	7b			
g5	60	94		
g6	11b			
g7	17			
h2	27			
h3	70			
h7	23	60	86b	94
h8	40	80c		

Index

abandonment of center, 53–54
a-file, development of knights to, 55–56
aimless development, 32–33
aimless exchanges, 157–58
algebraic notation, 17–18, 19–25
   symbols used in, 21
Anderssen-Schallop (1864), 41–42
a-pawns, 196–97
attacking, premature, 72–73
attraction, 271

back-rank mate, 271
bad move, probable, symbol for, 21
bad move, symbol for, 21
bad pieces, trades of, 169–70
battery, 271
bishops:
   enemy self-pins with N5 and, 115–16
   fianchettoed, see fianchetto
   flanking and self-trapping of, 124–25
   locked inside pawn chain, 36–37
   pawns and, 192–93
   playing to N5 to attack knights, 111–14
   queen-, blocking of, by queen-knight, 38–39
   sacrifice of, 38–39, 52, 59, 61, 75, 77, 88, 133, 135, 174, 201, 254, 258
   symbol for, 21
   unjustified attacks by, 117–20
blocking:
   of c-pawn at opening, 109–10
   of one's own forces, 34–35

of queen-bishop by queen-knight, 38–39
blunder, symbol for, 21
breakthrough, 102
brilliant move, symbol for, 21

Capablanca, John, 100–102, 202, 247
capitulation, premature, 267–68
captures, 128–87
   to automatically straighten pawn chains, 140–41
   away from the center, 138–39
   with check, 175–76
   with check automatically, 173–74
   delaying of, 146–47
   doubled pawns and, 162–64
   of e-pawns, 179–80
   letting opponent make first, 148–49
   with pawns, 142–43
   of pinned pieces, 165–66
   symbol for, 21
   unnecessary, 253–54
   with wrong piece, 136–37
Caro-Kann Defense, 160
castling:
   into danger, 85–86
   into a pin, 91–92
   into a skewer, 93–95
   delay of, 76–77
   forfeited due to check, 80–82
   and hanging pawns, 89–90
   kingside, symbol for, 21
   pawns and, 200–201
   queenside, moving rook to queen-one instead of, 83–84
   queenside, symbol for, 21
   on wrong side, 87–88

center:
    abandonment of, 53–54
    bringing of queen to, 60–61
    capturing away from, 138–39
    keeping king in, for endgame,
        98–102
    surrender of, to enemy queen,
        62–64
    trapping of king in, 78–79
center pawn roller, 54
center pawns, 34
cheap shots, 230–31
check, 271
    automatically with captures,
        173–74
    castling forfeited due to, 80–82
    missed captures with, 175–76
    pins created to block, 236–37
    pointless, 228–29
    symbol for, 21
checkmate, 271
    symbol for, 21
coffeehouse chess, 230–31
combination, 271
connecting rooks, failure in, 96–97
corridor mate, 271
counterattack, 271
counterplay, avoiding unnecessary,
        261–62
c-pawns, blocked at opening,
        109–10
cutoff, missing of, 217–18

decoy, 271
deflection, 271
descriptive notation, 17–18, 25–27
desperado, 271
developed pieces, undeveloped
        pieces traded for, 155–56
development:
    aimless, 32–33
    falling behind in, 30–31
    of knights only to second rank,
        57–59
    of knights to edge, 55–56
direct attack, 271
discovery, 47, 97, 112, 172, 231, 271

double check, 271
doubled pawns, 162–64, 194–95
double threat, 191, 216, 244, 271
Dragon Sicilian, 119–20
duplication of opponent's moves,
        74–75

edge files (a-file, h-file),
        development of knights to,
        55–56
endgame, keeping king in center
        for, 98–102
English Opening, 69
en prise, 272
e-pawns, capture of, 179–80
escape squares, 198–99
exchanges, 128–87
    aimless, 157–58
    allowing for, of weaknesses of
        opponent, 171–73
    avoidance of, 130–31, 159–61
    of bad pieces, 169–70
    of developed pieces for
        undeveloped ones, 155–56
    files surrendered by, 150–52
    and freeing your opponent's
        game, 167–68
    to lessen material, 185–87
    of pawns vs. pieces, 132–35
    of queens, 183–84
    tense situations and, 144–45
    when behind in material, 128–29

failure to compete, 267–68
fianchetto, 124, 125
    failure to complete, 121–23
    surrendering to win pawn,
        177–78
file conversions, from algebraic
        notation to descriptive
        notation, 26
files, trading and surrenders of,
        150–52
Fischer, Bobby, 49–50, 247
flanking, and self-trapping of
        bishops, 124–25

fork, 41, 56, 61, 65–69, 105, 108, 122, 123, 125, 139, 176, 182, 199, 221, 264, 272
fork tricks, missing of, 65–69
f-pawns:
  not moving, 106–8
  unwise moves of, 103–5
French Defense, 33, 36, 169

gaining time, 64, 107, 118, 119, 120
gambit, 272
general playing errors, 219–70
good move, probable, symbol for, 21
good move, symbol for, 21
Gurgenidze-Tal (1958), 71

h-file, development of knights to, 55–56
h-pawns, 196–97

in-between move, 272
initiative:
  slipping of, 70–71
  trading and, 159–61
interference, 272

jettison, 272
Joyce-Ross (1977), 81

Keres-Winter (1935), 31
king:
  activation of, 210–11
  castled, pawns and, 200–201
  in center for endgame, 98–102
  symbol for, 21
  trapping of, in center, 78–79
king hunt, 272
kings, oppositional relationship between, 208–9
kingside attack, 272

kingside castling, symbol for, 21
knights:
  bishops attacking, from N-5, 111–14
  developed only to second rank, 57–59
  development of, to edge, 55–56
  queen-, blocking queen-bishop with, 38–39
  sacrifice of, 31, 47, 67, 68, 69, 71, 112, 156, 195
  symbol for, 21

Lasker, Emanuel, 86–87, 221–23
Lasker-Englund (1913), 86–87
Letelier-Fischer (1960), 49–50
lines, obstructed by pawns, 142–43
locking of bishops inside pawn chain, 36–37
lost games, counterchances sought in, 267–68

McConnell-Morphy (1850), 51–52
majority of pawns, mobilizing of, 202–3
making luft, 198–99
Marache-Morphy (1857), 45–47
material:
  avoidance of trades when ahead in, 130–31
  capturing unnecessary, 253–54
  clinging to, 247–48
  trades to lessen, 185–87
  trading when behind in, 128–29
mating attack, 31, 39, 42, 50, 58, 71, 75, 79, 82, 84, 88, 137, 158, 197, 201, 248, 272
mating net, 59, 86, 97, 131, 152, 178, 184, 227, 240, 242, 272
Meek-Morphy (1855), 43–44
Merenyi-Capablanca (1928), 98–102
Morphy, Alonzo, 248
Morphy, Paul, 43–44, 45–47, 51–52, 84, 248
Morphy-Morphy (1849), 248

moves:
  duplicating of opponent's, 74–75
  of f-pawn, 103–5
  instant, time forfeit and, 232–33
  quick, 234–35
  of same piece several times,
    45–47
  too many pawns, 48–52
moves to, symbol for, 21
multiple threats, 52

N5 square:
  creating enemy self-pins from,
    115–16
  playing bishops to, 111–14

openings, blocking c-pawns in,
    109–10
opponent:
  allowed to camp out in one's
    position, 238–42
  allowing trades of bad pieces by,
    169–70
  allowing trades of weak pieces
    by, 171–72
  duplicating moves of, 74–75
  encouraging mistakes by, 263–64
  first captures allowed for, 148–49
  time forfeit and, 232–33
  trading to free game of, 167–68
opposition, 129, 203, 208–9
overload, 113, 272
overusing the queen, 40–44

Pandolfini-Morrison (1964), 78–79
pawns:
  bishops and, 192–93
  bishops locked behind chain of,
    36–37
  c-, blocking of, in opening,
    109–10
  capturing automatically to
    straighten, 140–41
  capturing with, 142–43
  castled king shielded by, 200–201

center, 34, 54
doubled, 194–95
doubled, created by captures,
    162–64
driving back bishops with, 117–20
e-, capture of, 179–80
f-, not moving, 106–8
f-, unwise moves of, 103–5
grabbing of, 251–52
heedless moving of, 190–91
hung by castling, 89–90
mobilizing majority of, 202–3
moving too many of, 48–52
pieces traded instead of, 134–35
rook-, 196–97
surrendering fianchettoed
    bishops for, 177–78
symbol for, 21
traded instead of pieces, 132–33
pieces:
  multiple moves of one, 45–47
  pawns traded instead of, 132–33
  traded instead of pawns, 134–35
  using wrong, to capture, 136–37
  vulnerable, 243–44
  weak, allowing opponent to
    trade, 171–73
piling on, 272
  vs. capture of pinned pieces,
    165–66
pin overload, 272
pins, 43, 44, 122, 141, 145, 180, 195,
    237, 258, 262, 272
  capture vs. piling on, 165–66
  castling into, 91–92
  created to block checks, 236–37
  self-, created by bishops, 115–16
plans:
  playing without, 220–23
  rigid, 224–27
pointless checks, 228–29
position, enemy forces in, 238–42
Potemkin-Alekhine (1912), 82
premature attacking, 72–73
premature capitulation, 267–68
premature resignation, 269–70
probably a bad move, symbol
    for, 21

probably a good move, symbol for, 21
promotion, 147, 161, 174, 205, 233, 235, 268, 270, 272

Q4 square, queen recaptures and, 181–82
queen-bishop, blocked by queen-knight, 38–39
queen-knight, blocking queen-bishop with, 38–39
queens:
  avoiding trade of, 183–84
  bringing of, to assailable center square, 60–61
  enemy, surrender of center to, 62–64
  making too many, 249–50
  overuse of, 40–44
  recapturing with, on Q4, 181–82
  sacrifice of, 42, 50, 82, 84, 86, 131, 161, 178, 184, 199, 240, 244, 250, 258, 262
  symbol for, 21
Queen's Gambit Declined, 36
queenside, castling, 83–84
  symbol for, 21
quick moves, 234–35

rank conversions, from algebraic notation to descriptive notation, 26–27
recaptures, 128–87
  with queen to Q4, 181–82
removing the defender, 272
removing the guard, 272
resignation, premature, 269–70
rook files, development of knights to, 55–56
rook-pawns, 196–97
rooks:
  automatic oppositions of, 153–54
  direct-line power of, 217–18
  failure to connect, 96–97
  moving to queen-one instead of castling queenside, 83–84

moving wrong, 212–13
passive, 214–16
sacrifice of, 79, 84, 97, 102, 105, 108, 145, 178, 227, 231, 262, 264
symbol for, 21
see also castling
Ruy Lopez, 68

sacrifices, 272
  of bishop, 38–39, 52, 59, 61, 75, 77, 88, 133, 135, 174, 201, 254, 258
  declined out of fear, 257–58
  of knight, 31, 47, 67, 68, 69, 71, 112, 156, 195
  of queen, 42, 50, 82, 84, 86, 131, 161, 178, 184, 199, 240, 244, 250, 258, 262
  of rook, 79, 84, 97, 102, 105, 108, 145, 178, 227, 231, 262, 264
  sham vs. true, 255–56
sacrifice squares, 277
saving, 272
Scholar's Mate, 73
second rank, development of knights to, 57–59
self-blocking, 34–35
self-pins, enemy, created by bishops, 115–16
self-trapping, 245–46
  and flanking of bishops, 124–25
seventh rank, 206–7
shut-off, 272
Sicilian Defense, 64, 92, 241
simplification, 133, 135
skewers, 46, 77, 149, 215, 266, 272
  castling into, 93–95
smothered mate, 273
Speyer-Couvee, 239–40
squares, 20
  obstructed by pawns, 142–43
stalemate, 145, 250, 254, 259–60, 273
strategy, 273
support mate, 273
symbols in algebraic notation, 21

tactics, 273
tactics glossary, 271–73
tactics index, 275–76
Tarrasch, Siegbert, 221–23
Tarrasch-Lasker (1908), 221–23
technique, 273
threats, multiple, 52
time forfeit, and instant moves,
    232–33
trades, avoidance of, 130–31
trading:
  aimless, 157–58
  allowing for, of weaknesses of
      opponent, 171–73
  avoidance of, 159–61
  of bad pieces, 169–70
  of developed pieces for
      undeveloped ones, 155–56
  files surrendered by, 150–52
  and freeing your opponent's
      game, 167–68
  to lessen material, 185–87
  of pawns vs. pieces, 132–35
  of queens, 183–84
  tense situations and, 144–45
  when behind in material, 128–29
trapped pieces, 273
  getting most out of, 265–66

trapping, 213, 252, 273
  of king in center, 78–79
  self-, 245–46
two-square options, 204–5

undermining, 114, 156, 211, 273
underpromotion, 270, 273
undeveloped pieces, developed
    pieces traded for, 155–56
unguarding, 90
unnecessary captures, 253–54
unnecessary checks, 228–29
unpin, 256, 273

vulnerable pieces, 243–44

weak pieces, trades of, 171–72
winning the exchange, 273

x-ray, 273

zugzwang, 273
zwischenzug, 273

About the Author

Bruce Pandolfini is the author of seventeen instructional chess books, including *Chess Thinking; Chess Target Practice; More Chess Openings: Traps and Zaps 2; Beginning Chess; Pandolfini's Chess Complete; Chessercizes; More Chessercizes; Checkmate!; Principles of the New Chess; Pandolfini's Endgame Course; Russian Chess; The ABC's of Chess; Let's Play Chess; Kasparov's Winning Chess Tactics; One-Move Chess by the Champions; Chess Openings: Traps and Zaps; Square One;* and *Weapons of Chess.* He is also the editor of the distinguished anthologies *The Best of Chess Life & Review,* Volumes I and II, and has produced, with David MacEnuity, two instructional videotapes, *Understanding Chess* and *Opening Principles.*

Bruce was the chief commentator at the New York half of the 1990 Kasparov-Karpov World Chess Championship, and in 1990 was head coach of the United States Team in the World Youth Chess Championships in Wisconsin. Perhaps the most experienced chess teacher in North America, he is co-founder, with Faneuil Adams, of the Manhattan Chess Club School and is the director of the New York City Schools Program. Bruce's most famous student, six-time National Scholastic Champion Joshua Waitzkin, is the subject of Fred Waitzkin's acclaimed book *Searching for Bobby Fischer* and of the movie of the same name. Bruce Pandolfini lives in New York City.